W9-BFA-036

MATHEMATICAL INVESTIGATIONS

BOOK ONE

A Series of Situational Lessons

Geometry • Patterns

Operations Research

Photography • Genetics

Randall Souviney

Murray Britt

Salvi Gargiulo

Peter Hughes

DALE SEYMOUR PUBLICATIONS

This U.S. edition is adapted from *Investigations in Mathematics* by
M. Britt, S.V. Gargiulo, and P. Hughes (Auckland, New Zealand:
New House Publishers, 1988).

Cover design: Rachel Gage
Illustrations: Edith Allgood (for Dale Seymour Publications); Felicity Blake
and Warren Mahy (for New House Publishers)

Copyright © 1990, 1988 by Randall Souviney, Murray Britt,
Salvi Gargiulo, and Peter Hughes. All rights reserved. Printed in the
United States of America. Published simultaneously in Canada.

Limited reproduction permission: The publisher grants permission to
individual teachers who have purchased this book to reproduce the
investigations as needed for use with their own students. Reproduction
for an entire school district or for commercial use is prohibited.

Order number DS01013
ISBN 0-86651-502-X

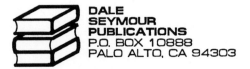
DALE
SEYMOUR
PUBLICATIONS
P.O. BOX 10888
PALO ALTO, CA 94303

3 4 5 6 7 8 9 10 11 12-MA-95 94 93 92 91

CONTENTS

PREFACE

During a debate about whether to install the emergency number 911 in the county, a council member complained that in a panic, people would get confused looking for the *eleven* button! While it is not unusual to hear such a low opinion of the public's number sense, in fact most people use some level of mathematical thinking as they attempt to solve everyday problems.

For example, a woman planning to buy a house near San Francisco, California, noticed that newly constructed homes seemed to be less expensive the farther they were from the city center. Looking at a local real estate magazine, she made a table that listed the prices of three-bedroom houses and their distance from the city. From the pattern in the table, she found she could generally use distance from the city to predict the price of a house. Starting with the cost of a similar house close to the city, she simply subtracted $1500 per mile of distance from the city center.

What would cause a pattern like this one to occur? The answer is quite simple: Since material and labor costs are relatively constant throughout California, the consistent drop in housing costs that the woman observed is directly related to land cost. The value of land is based largely on what people are willing to pay. All other things being equal, commuting distance to work is a primary factor people consider when purchasing a home. Since jobs are often located near urban centers, people are willing to pay more to reduce their commuting time.

Of course, there are exceptions to the real-estate cost rule that this woman formulated. When the distance from the city exceeded 30 miles or so, the cost reduction leveled off, as it necessarily must; otherwise the price would eventually drop to zero. Nonetheless, what the woman discovered was a useful pattern that she could apply as she tried to choose a community in which to live.

As this example illustrates, sometimes we can better understand the phenomena we see in nature and society by using mathematical tools and reasoning. *Mathematical Investigations* is a series of three books for the secondary school level, designed to develop students' mathematical reasoning abilities in everyday situational lessons. In this Book One of the series, the investigations are grouped into five chapters, introducing fundamental mathematical ideas in the context of geometry, patterns, operations research, photography, and genetic inheritance. These topics were selected not only because they appeal to the interests of secondary students, but also because each provides unique opportunities to develop a specific approach to mathematical problem solving.

Each investigation involves one or more applications of algebra, geometry, graphing, counting, probability, and statistics in solving practical problems; at the same time, it teaches a kind of reasoning that cuts across all grade levels and many mathematical fields. By examining certain aspects of real-world situations while working on their own through a guided discovery process, students can develop confidence in using mathematics in their everyday lives, whether or not they intend to pursue a mathematics-based career.

These materials support a number of the recommendations made in the *Curriculum and Evaluation Standards for School Mathematics,* published in 1989 by the National Council of Teachers of Mathematics (NCTM), as well as the principles stated in state curriculum overviews such as California's *Mathematics Framework.* These documents recommend that mathematics be presented *not* as a collection of concepts and skills to be mastered, but rather as a variety of methods for investigating and thinking about problems. In this type of curriculum the students, rather than being passive absorbers of information, become more self-directed, taking an active role as they make conjectures, discover and abstract relationships from problem situations, verify assertions, reason and explain their reasoning, and generally construct their own meaning.

This book, then, bears little resemblance to a traditional mathematics textbook; neither is it one of the familiar collections of discrete supplementary activities that teachers can dole out for practice, extension, or review. Instead, this is a book of challenging, inter-connected situational lessons linked together in the sequences that we call *investigations.* Teaching notes at the beginning of each chapter explain the important mathematical and scientific generalizations to be presented. The investigations follow, each consisting of a series of questions, exercises, and increasingly more complex problems carefully sequenced to help students identify a solution strategy, which in turn leads them to important generalizations. Many of the questions require essay-type answers:

Explain her reasoning.

Explain why this would be true.

Why is this a losing strategy?

Explain how the diagram works.

Students may not be accustomed to writing long verbal answers for their math exercises, but expressing new concepts in their own words is a proven way to help them clarify their reasoning.

While the pages of this book are reproducible, they *cannot* be regarded as single-page handouts; each investigation, ranging from 2 to 9 pages, must be duplicated as a complete packet so that students can work through it from beginning to end. Within a given investigation, students will encounter special extension activities called "On Your Own" that generally involve independent experimentation or research, some of which may have to take place outside of class. Other special activities, termed "Class Investigations," are well-suited to small-group or whole-class work.

Throughout the investigations, students will learn to use such general problem-solving tools as *trying simpler cases, conducting experiments, looking for patterns, using the guess-and-check tactic, looking for symmetry,* and *using logical reasoning.* They also use more specific tools such as *constructing tables, making models, graphing data, drawing sketches, making systematic lists,* and *writing formulas* as they work to unravel the underlying relationships in a problem. Teachers should remind and encourage students to try one or more of these tools as they investigate each new problem situation. Additionally, it is assumed that students will have access to hand-held calculators at all times and will use them freely in the computation involved in these investigations.

A "Check-Up" quiz at the end of each chapter gives students a chance to check their understanding of the principles and procedures that they encountered in the investigations.

Because the concepts underlying these investigations are drawn from more than one area of mathematics, we have included in each book a collection of 35 KEYMATH concepts that students may need to review. As students work through the investigations, they will periodically see in the margin a small key symbol with a number inside, referring them to a particular KEYMATH concept. Teachers may want to have several sets of the KEYMATH section duplicated and available for student reference. Students who need help can turn to this section to find a brief discussion of the concept followed by a short set of practice exercises.

Answers for exercises and problems in both the investigations and the KEYMATH section are included at the end of the book.

CHAPTER ONE

GEOMETRY

TEACHING NOTES

Geometric concepts are often used in the description and solution of problems involving spatial relationships, ratio, proportion, and scales. This chapter presents three geometric investigations that ask students to maximize or minimize some factor under a specific set of conditions.

Investigation One • Symmetry

The area of a plane region is related to its symmetry. Given a fixed perimeter, the more lines of symmetry a region possesses, the greater its area. For a fixed perimeter, then, the area of a scalene triangle is less than the area of an equilateral triangle, which is less than that of a square, which is less than that of a circle. As they explore the implications of this principle, students investigate ways to design a building to minimize costs, as well as efficient ways to enclose fields with electric fencing and to design water pipes for maximum flow.

An interesting extension to this investigation involves the curious behavior of the "snowflake" invented in 1904 by the Swedish mathematician Helge von Koch.

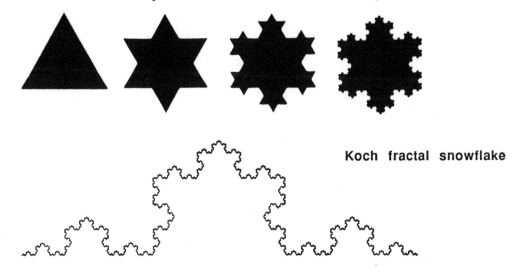

Koch fractal snowflake

The Koch snowflake starts with an equilateral triangle having sides of length 1. If we construct a new equilateral triangle on the middle third of each side of original triangle, with sides $1/3$ the length of the side of the larger triangle, the result is a six-pointed star. At the middle of each of the 12 sides of the star, we again construct equilateral triangles with sides $1/3$ the length of the next larger sides. Continuing this process an infinite number of times gives a simple closed figure that Benoit Mandelbrot called a *fractal*—a figure whose edge has the same shape regardless of the scale (i.e., how much it is magnified). The new triangles formed by this process are always small enough to avoid bumping into each other on their way to infinity. The snowflake will fall entirely within the circle that inscribes the original triangle and therefore has less area than the circle. (Note that the snowflake also has fewer lines of symmetry than the circle.) We can calculate the perimeter:

$$3 \times \frac{4}{3} \times \frac{4}{3} \times \frac{4}{3} \cdots = \infty$$

The Koch snowflake is a figure of finite area and infinite perimeter!

Interested students can invent their own "snowflakes"; for example, they might draw a similar series of figures based on a square by constructing equilateral triangles with sides $1/3$ the length of the sides of the square, and then try to calculate the perimeter of their figure ($4 \times \frac{4}{3} \times \frac{4}{3} \times \frac{4}{3} \cdots = \infty$).

Investigation Two • Biology

The volume of a three-dimensional figure is related to its symmetry. Given a fixed surface area, the more planes of symmetry a figure possesses, the greater its volume. For a fixed surface area, then, the volume of a pyramid is less than that of a cube, which is less than that of a cylinder, which is less than that of a sphere. Students investigate the effect that the shape of an object has on its ability to maintain heat (i.e., the greater the surface area, the faster the object loses heat to the environment), relating the concept to the melting of ice, the cooling of beverages by refrigeration, and the loss of body heat (with its attendant risk of hypothermia).

Investigation Three • Container Design

Students work to design cans with the minimum surface area—and thus minimum material costs—for a given volume. They use tables to list the results of their trial solutions. Using the fact that the surface area of a cylinder is minimized for a given volume when the height equals the diameter ($h = 2r$), students investigate the efficiency of different can designs.

Investigation One

Symmetry

1 **a** Two factors that influence the cost of building a house are the floor area and the perimeter of the house. Explain why.

  b Nick and Alan want to know whether the design shown here is the cheapest way to build a beach house with a floor area of 64 m².

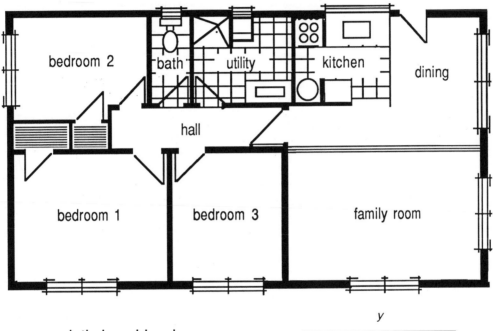

They approach their problem by drawing a set of rectangles of different shapes, all with the area 64 unit².

y

x | $A = 64$

The perimeter is *P* units.

c **i** Complete the table.
  ii What perimeter would result in the cheapest design?

x	y	P
1	64	130
2		
4		
8		
16		
32		
64		

d As a check, Nick now draws a set of rectangles, each with a perimeter of 32 units.

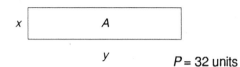

$P = 32$ units

i Complete the table.
ii Which rectangle has the *maximum* area?

x	y	A
0	16	0
2	14	28
4		
6		
8		
10		
12		
14		
16		

e What kind of rectangle is described by the solution to **c** and to **d**?

f The floor area for the house shown here is about 81 m².

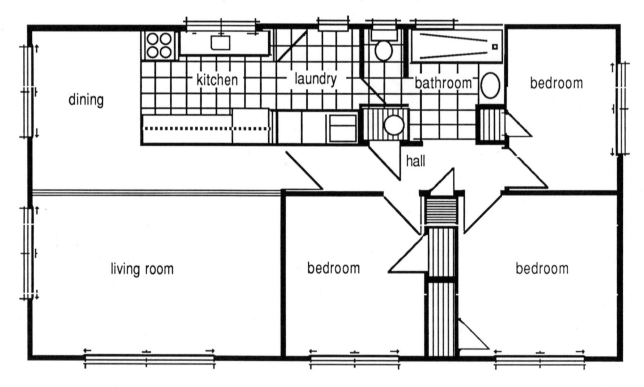

i Suggest a design for a house that has an 81 m² floor area with the minimum perimeter for that area.
ii What should the perimeter be?

g A house with a rectangular floor plan is designed with a perimeter of 40 m.
i What shape should the plan be to provide a maximum floor area?
ii What is the maximum floor area?

2 Henry thinks that ABCD is the largest rectangle he can draw inside the circle.

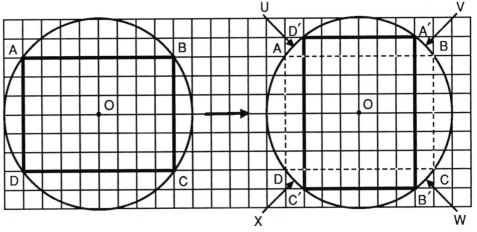

a What is the area of ABCD?

b Susan rotates ABCD 90° clockwise about O to give A'B'C'D'. She then draws the square that touches the circle at points U, V, W, and X.
   i In the diagram, draw the square UVWX.
   ii Find the area of this square by counting the unit squares.

c **i** What is the area of the largest rectangle that can be drawn inside the circle?
   ii How do you know it is the largest?

18 **d** **i** In the diagram at right, draw the largest triangle that will fit inside the semicircle.
   ii Calculate the area of the triangle.
   iii Explain why this triangle is the largest one possible.

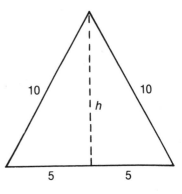

3 Brian draws an isosceles triangle with a perimeter of 30 units.

24

a Use the Pythagorean theorem to explain why $h = \sqrt{135}$.

b Show that the area of Brian's triangle is about 34.86 units².

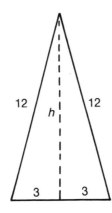

c Of all isosceles triangles with a perimeter of 30 units, Brian predicts that the one with maximum area is equilateral. Suggest why he might think this is true.

1 d i Complete the table. (Round to two decimal places where necessary.)

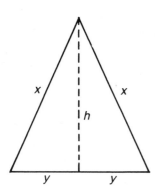

x	y	h	Area
14	1	$\sqrt{195}$	
13			
12	3	$\sqrt{135}$	34.86
11			
10	5		
9			
8			
7			

ii Is Brian's prediction correct?

e Explain why $7.5 < x < 15$.

f A triangle has a fixed area. What shape will the triangle be to get a *minimum* perimeter?

4 The perimeter of each of these triangles is 24 units.

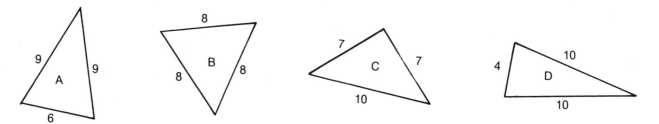

Which one has the *maximum* area? Explain your answer.

ON YOUR OWN

1 Cut a circular disk from a piece of paper. Make the radius 12 cm.

2 Fold the disk to form a triangle with the maximum perimeter.

3 Find the area of the triangle.

5 Mirisa has 360 m of electric fencing to enclose her cows in a field. She decides to use either an equilateral triangle or a square design.

a She predicts that the square will enclose more grass. Explain what her reasoning must be.

b Check her prediction by calculating the areas of the triangle and the square. (Round to two significant figures.)

c Would a regular pentagon with a perimeter of 360 m be an even better solution? Explain your answer.

d For a regular hexagon with a perimeter of 360 m, calculate the following:
  i the area of △ABC. (Do not round yet.)
  ii the area of the hexagon. (Round to two significant figures.)

e Of the four designs shown, which is the best? Explain your answer.

6 Robyn designs two place mats, one a square and one a circle, each with a perimeter of 124 cm.

a Predict which will have the larger area.

b **i** Find the radius of a circle with a perimeter of 124 cm. (Do not round yet.)
  ii Find the area of the circle. (Round sensibly.)

c Was your prediction correct?

7 Nita, an architect, is commissioned to design a 121 m² building with a concrete path around it. She makes two designs, one square and the other a circle. To reduce the cost of the path, she wants to know which building design has the shorter perimeter.

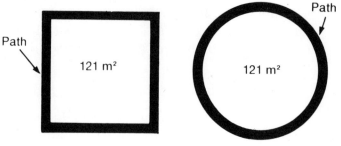

a Predict which design has the shorter perimeter.

b Show that the perimeter of the square is 44 m.

c i Find the radius of the circle. (Do not round yet.)
   ii Find the circumference of the circle. (Round sensibly.)

d Was your prediction correct?

8 The following shapes A, B, and C have the same area.

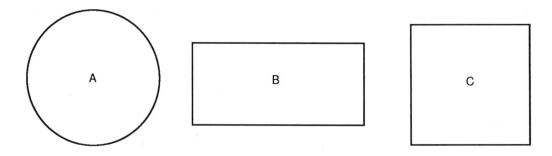

a Which has the minimum perimeter?

b Which has the maximum perimeter?

Explain your answers.

9 Maria thinks that the solution to maximum or minimum problems is usually the shape with the most lines of symmetry.

35

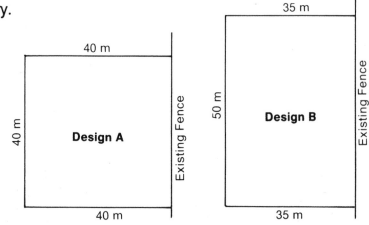

a Is Maria's principle a good one?

b Alex has 120 m of electric fencing. He wants to enclose a rectangle of grass having the maximum possible area. He uses an existing fence for one side of the enclosure. Does his Design A use Maria's principle?

c Find the area of grass enclosed
   i by Design A.
   ii by Design B.

d Does Maria's principle work in Design B? Explain your answer.

e Suggest a design for the rectangle with the maximum area that can be enclosed with 120 m of fencing, using the existing fence.

ON YOUR OWN

Make a loop out of inelastic string.
(The loop's perimeter is fixed.)

1   With your loop, make various shapes over graph paper and, by counting squares, find the areas enclosed.

2   What is the shape of the loop with the maximum area? Why is this result predictable?

10   Three lengths of sheet metal, each with a width of 240 mm, are folded to make pipes. Their cross sections are shown here.

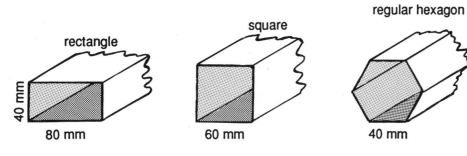

rectangle

square

regular hexagon

40 mm

80 mm

60 mm

40 mm

a   Which of the pipes will allow the greatest flow of water? Explain your answer.

b   Why do you suppose water spouts are usually cylindrical?

c   A length of sheet metal with a width of 30 cm is folded to make a water course. Which of the following designs will allow the greater flow of water? The cross section of Design A is half a square. The cross section of Design B is half a regular hexagon.

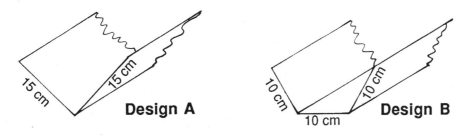

15 cm   15 cm   **Design A**

10 cm   10 cm   **Design B**

10 cm

d   Design a water course that will allow for greater flow than either Design A or Design B.

11 Regan wants to design a cuboid (a container with rectangular sides) for 1 liter (1000 cm³) of apple juice.

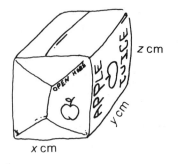

a Using Maria's principle (problem 9), guess what shape would make the cheapest packaging—that is, would have the minimum surface area.

b What are dimensions of the container in a?

c i Complete the table for cuboids with a volume of 1000 cm³. Extend the table as necessary.

(T = total surface area in cm²)

x	y	z	2xy	2xz	2yz	T (cm²)
1	1	1000	2	2000	2000	4002
1	2	500				
1	5	200				
1	10	100				
2	2					
⋮	⋮					

ii Does your table confirm Maria's principle?

d i A piece of cardboard with an area of 600 cm² is available to make a cuboid. Predict the shape that has the *maximum* volume.

ii Confirm your prediction, if you can, by designing some boxes with a surface area of 600 cm².

ON YOUR OWN

A carton is designed to hold 4000 cm³ of strawberries. It has no top.

1 Explain why the carton that uses the minimum amount of cardboard or other material is *not* a cube.

2 Find the design that uses the minimum amount of cardboard by designing a series of cartons.

12 A ball and an egg have the same volume.

   a Which has the smaller surface area?

   b Would an egg producer be advised to look for chickens that lay spherical eggs? Explain your answer.

   c Why do you suppose eggs are generally not spherical?

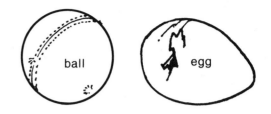

13 Here are three possible designs for submarines, shown in cross section. The areas are roughly equal.

Design A   **Design B**   **Design C**

Which do you suspect is the best design for withstanding the enormous water pressure at great depths? Explain your reasoning.

Investigation Two

Biology

1   A block of ice consists of three cubes frozen together. Thomas wonders whether the ice will melt more quickly if he breaks the block into three cubes.

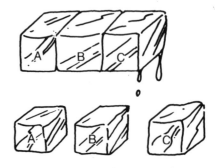

a   i   Complete the table.

| | Number of Faces Exposed to Heat | | | |
	Block A	Block B	Block C	Total
Before breaking block	5			
After breaking block	6			

   ii   What is the answer to Thomas's question?

b   Thomas uses 27 small cubes of ice to build a large block measuring $3 \times 3 \times 3$. He wonders if this large block will melt more slowly than the 27 cubes kept separate from each other.

   i   Show that the 27 cubes kept separate have 162 faces exposed.
   ii   Show that in the large block, a total of 54 small cube faces are exposed.
   iii   Thomas concludes the large block will melt much more slowly than the 27 separate cubes. Is he correct? Explain your answer.

c   Thomas has to deliver eight large cubes of ice to a school picnic. Unfortunately the freezer motor on his truck has broken down, so he decides to arrange the eight blocks together in order to minimize the melting on his delivery run. By trying various arrangements of the blocks, work out the *best* way for Thomas to stack the ice. Comment on any symmetry you notice in your answer.

2 Suppose a chunk of ice contains 20 liters of water. What is the best shape for the ice to minimize the speed of melting? Use a symmetry explanation.

3 A family takes a cooler full of soft drinks to the beach. They plan to add ice to the cooler to keep the drinks cold.

   a Would a single block of ice or crushed ice be better? Explain why.

   b The family is going camping for a long holiday weekend with no access to a refrigerator. They want to keep their meat in a cooler. In this case, would a block of ice or crushed ice be better? Explain why.

4 Kool Kustomers plans to tow a 100 000 000 ton iceberg from Antarctica to Saudi Arabia as a fresh water supply, while the Top Ice Company plans to tow four icebergs, each weighing 25 000 000 tons. Decide which company has the better plan to supply fresh water and explain your reasoning.

5 Jenny plans to make 1 L of ice from water as quickly as possible. She can either use a liter container in the shape of a cube or make 50 smaller cubes of 20 ml each. Which should she do? Explain your answer.

6 A mother and her small son fall out of their boat into cold water. They are wearing life jackets, so drowning is not a danger. However, the mother is aware of the danger of excessive heat loss (hypothermia).

   a For whom is the risk of hypothermia greater?

   b Explain why you believe your answer to **a** is correct.

c The mother tells her son to bring his knees up close to his body to help reduce the heat loss. Is this a sensible strategy? Explain your answer.

Hypothermia

What is it?

Hypothermia means a lowered deep-body temperature. It is a potentially dangerous condition. In cold air or cold water, the skin and external tissues become cooled very rapidly. However, it takes 10–15 minutes before the temperature of the heart and brain begins to cool. Intense shivering occurs in a futile attempt to increase the body's heat production and counteract the large heat loss. Decreased consciousness occurs when the deep-body temperature falls from the normal 37° C (98.6° F) to approximately 30°–32° C (86°–90° F). Heart failure is the usual cause of death when deep-body temperature cools to below 30° C (86° F).

Survival in the water

The body surrenders its heat to water many times more quickly than to air of the same temperature, and it is often possible to stabilize body temperature once you are out of the water. Therefore, if possible, get on top of an overturned boat or any wreckage that is available. If there are no such objects, you are left with two alternatives.

H.E.L.P. (Heat Escape Lessening Posture)

• Keep head out of water, including back of head.

• Place arms against sides, chest, and life jacket.

• Cross lower legs, raising knees as much as waves and stability permit, but keeping the knees together.

HUDDLE (Two or more people huddled together)

• Keep heads out of water, including back of heads.

• Hug each other tightly.

• Maintain maximum body contact, especially at the chest, reducing heat loss.

• Keep legs intertwined as much as possible.

• Talk to maintain morale.

ON YOUR OWN

1 Put one small bottle and one large bottle of orange juice in the refrigerator at the same time.

   a Predict which bottle will cool more quickly.

   b Check your prediction by leaving the bottles in the refrigerator for a while and then tasting each.

2 A small and a large saucepan of water are each brought to a boil.

   a Predict which saucepan will cool more quickly.

   b Check your prediction by experiment.

7 "Blue Ice" freezer packs are frozen overnight for use in a cooler the next day. Would eight packs weighing 200 g each or one pack weighing 1600 g be better for keeping the food and drink cool on a picnic? Explain your answer.

8 a Find out how sweating helps keep people cool on hot days.

   b A father on the beach is sweating, but notices that his small daughter is not. What is a possible explanation for why this happens?

9 Five mountaineers are trapped in a mountain hut without any heating. What should they do to minimize the risk of dying from hypothermia? Explain your answer.

10 You have brought soda pop to the beach. A small bottle and a large bottle of similar shape are taken from the cooler and left by accident in the sun. After 30 minutes, which bottle would you choose to drink from? Explain why.

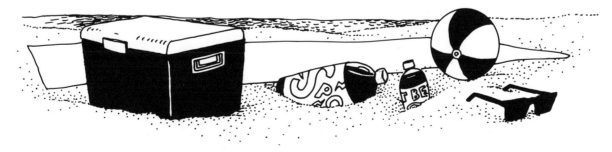

11 Keri has nine heat storage bricks (cubes)
that are heated to the same temperature.
She packs eight bricks together to form
a large cube, 20 cm × 20 cm × 20 cm.

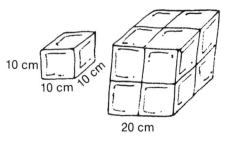

a   Complete the table. (The heat energy in each brick is 6000 heat units.)

	Number of Bricks	Heat Units
Small cube	1	6000
Large cube	8	

b   After making several observations, Keri notices that the bricks lose heat
at the rate of 1 heat unit per minute for every square centimeter of
exposed surface. Complete the table.

	Surface Area (cm²)	Heat Loss in One Minute (Units)
Small cube	600	
Large cube		

c   Show that in one minute:
   i   the small cube loses 10% of its heat.
   ii the large cube loses 5% of its heat.

d   Explain why large objects cool less quickly than similar small objects.

e   Explain why children are more likely to suffer from exposure to cold
than adults.

f   A beached whale is more likely to die through overheating than a
beached dolphin. Explain why.

ON YOUR OWN

Suppose you have heat storage bricks like those described in problem 11. Pack them together in blocks, making pairs of similar shape but different size, and test for heat losses per cm² per minute.

Check that the percentage heat loss in your larger object is less than in your smaller object.

12 **a** Suppose that a mouse weighing 50 g must eat 25 g of food a day to stay alive. Mark is a 14-year-old boy who weighs 50 kg. Suppose Mark eats at the same rate as the mouse. Complete the table to show how much food he would eat in a day.

	Weight	Food Intake
Mouse	50 g	25 g
Mark	50 kg	

b How much, roughly, does a 50-kg human actually eat per day?

c Why do you suppose the answers to **a** and **b** are so different?

d i In the graph below are four possible curves representing the weight of mammals (W) in relation to the percentage of their weight (P) they must eat each day to survive. Which curve best represents the relationship? Explain your answer.

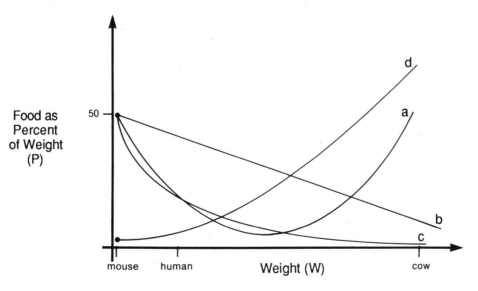

ii Why is it impossible for mammals the size of beetles to exist?

13 Lizards can hardly move when they are cold.

 a Find out why this occurs.

 b A small lizard and a large lizard wake up on a rock together. As the sun warms them up, they become active. Which lizard do you think will become active first?

 c At nightfall, which lizard could remain active longer?

14 A lump of sugar is put in a solution of yeast. The yeast acts on the sugar to produce alcohol and carbon dioxide.

 a A chemist says that to speed up the reaction, the sugar lump should have been crushed. Explain her reasoning.

 b Another chemist claims that stirring the sugar to dissolve it is an even better strategy. Explain why this would be true.

15 The two pieces of candy pictured at right are made from the same ingredients and. contain equal amounts. Which do you think would dissolve more quickly in your mouth? Explain your answer.

A   B

ON YOUR OWN

Detergents break down fats into very small droplets. This process is called *emulsifying*.

 1 Explain how this would help to clean hair. (Shampoos are basically detergents despite their exotic names.)

 2 Find out how soaps work (they do *not* work like detergents).

 3 Fats that we eat are emulsified by bile. Find out how bile helps us digest fats in our food.

Investigation Three

Container Design

1 Calculate the volume of the can shown here. (Round sensibly.)

2 Jackie wants to design a can to hold 333 ml.

a Explain why $\pi r^2 h = 333$.

b Explain why the surface area of the can, S, is given by $S = 2\pi r^2 + 2\pi rh$.

c Jackie decides to use a height of 11.2 cm.
  i Work out the radius. (Do not round yet.)
  ii Work out the surface area of the can. (Round sensibly.)

d Jackie wants to find a design for the 333 ml can that will minimize the cost of the can (by minimizing the surface area). Complete the tables. (Round the surface area columns sensibly.)

i

h (cm)	r (cm)	S (cm²)
15.0		
12.5		
10.0		
7.5		
5.0		

ii

h (cm)	r (cm)	S (cm²)
4.5		
3.6		
2.8		
2.4		
1.2		

e Jackie's friend Luis suggests that cylinders with minimum surface area (for a given volume) will also have the greatest symmetry.
  i Describe the relationship between the diameter and height of a cylinder that provides the minimum surface area for a given volume.
  ii Analyze the completed tables in **d** to check your conclusion.

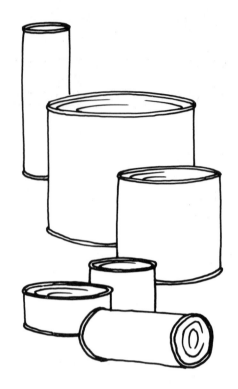

3   Jackie must design a can that will hold 821 cm³.

   a   By preparing tables like those in problem **2d**, design a set of possible can shapes.

   b   For the optimal can (where the surface area is minimal), does $h = 2r$? ($2r$ = diameter)

4 a   Show that the volume of a can with *minimum* surface area, S, is represented by the formula $V = 2\pi r^3$.

   b   Complete the table. (Round S to the nearest cm².)

V	r (cm)	S (cm²)
1000 ml		
2000 ml		
3.0 L		
4.0 L		
5.8 L		

ON YOUR OWN

1   Design a can to hold 1430 cm³ with the minimum surface area. (Does $h = 2r$?)

2   Measure the radii and heights of various cans in your home. Is their design optimal? If not, why not?

5   Jackie now must design a can to hold 4.000 L (4000 cm³) of water. The can will have no lid.

   a   Jackie suspects that there is a simple rule involving r and h that might be used to make cans without lids from the minimum amount of material. What do you think the rule is?

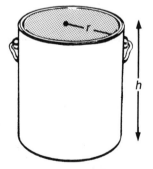

   b   If $h = 41.0$ cm, work out the following:
      i   the radius. (Do not round yet.)
      ii the surface area of the can. (Round sensibly.)

c If *S* is the area of sheet metal used to make the can, explain why $S = \pi r^2 + 2\pi rh$.

d Complete the tables. (Round the *S* columns sensibly.)

i

h (cm)	*r* (cm)	*S* (cm²)
18.2		
14.8		
12.7		
10.8		
9.7		

ii

h (cm)	*r* (cm)	*S* (cm²)
8.6		
7.9		
6.3		
4.8		
2.6		

e Do your completed tables confirm the rule you proposed in **a**?

6 a Show that for cans without lids and with *minimum* surface area, the volume is represented by the formula $V = \pi r^3$.

b Complete the table at the right. (Round *S* to the nearest cm².)

V	*r* (cm)	*S* (cm²)
5000 ml		
6.0 L		
6.7 L		
5.0 L		
5.8 L		
500 ml		

7 a David rolls a piece of paper to make a cylinder.
  i Find the radius of the cylinder. (Do not round yet.)
  ii Find the volume of the cylinder. (Round sensibly.)

b Moana boasts that she can make a cylinder of larger volume from the same piece of paper.
  i Find the volume of Moana's new cylinder.
  ii Is Moana correct?

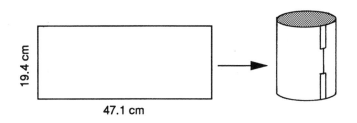

19.4 cm

47.1 cm

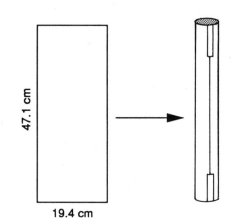

47.1 cm

19.4 cm

c Which of the following cylinders will have the greater volume? Check your prediction by calculation.

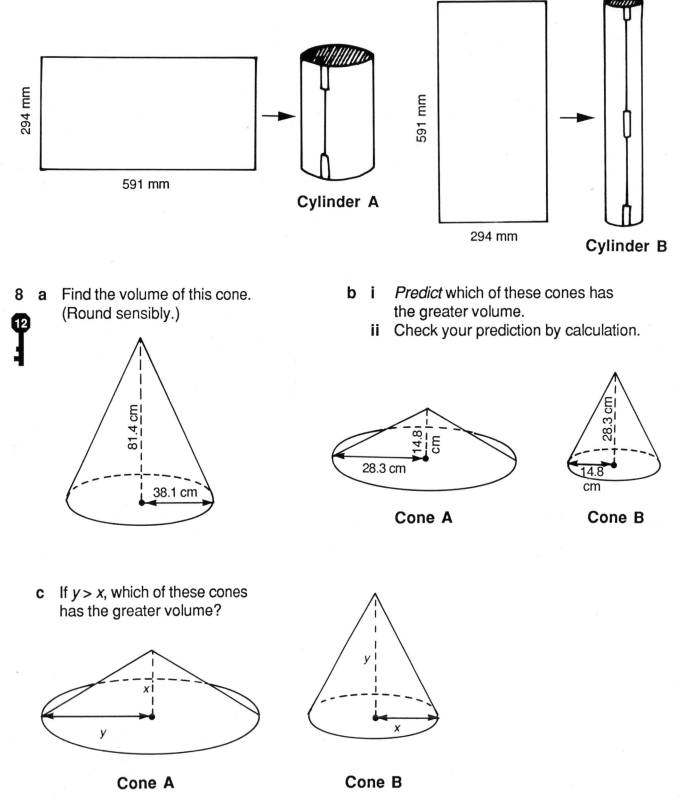

294 mm

591 mm

Cylinder A

591 mm

294 mm

Cylinder B

8 a Find the volume of this cone. (Round sensibly.)

81.4 cm

38.1 cm

b i *Predict* which of these cones has the greater volume.

ii Check your prediction by calculation.

14.8 cm

28.3 cm

Cone A

28.3 cm

14.8 cm

Cone B

c If $y > x$, which of these cones has the greater volume?

x

y

Cone A

y

x

Cone B

ON YOUR OWN

1   Use a calculator to design several cones that can hold 56.8 L of water.

2   Which of your designs is best? Explain why.

CLASS INVESTIGATION

1   Eli folds a circular filter paper into a cone-shaped funnel as shown in the diagram.

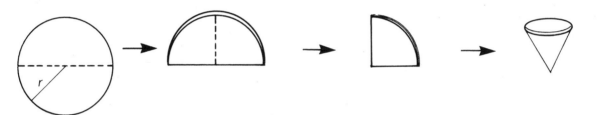

a   Fold a circular paper disk the same way.
   i   Explain why the circumference of the funnel is half the circumference of the circular filter paper.

   ii   Why is the radius of the funnel equal to $\frac{r}{2}$?

b   The following diagram shows a vertical cross section through the center of the funnel.

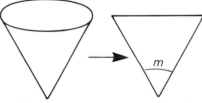

Explain why the cross section is an equilateral triangle.

c   i   What is the size of angle m?
   ii   How should m affect the design of the glass filter funnels that are manufactured for use in science laboratories and for coffee filters? Check this design feature on a variety of filter funnels.

CHECK-UP

1   The park commission has 300.0 m of fencing to fence off an area for a children's playground.

    a Complete the table to show the dimensions that yield the maximum area for each playground design.

Design Shape	Number of Sides	Length of Sides (m)
Triangle		
Quadrilateral		
Pentagon		
Hexagon		

    b **i** The park commission eventually decides to make the playground circular. Why do you think they chose a circular design?

        ii Find the radius of the circle and the area enclosed by the 300.0 m fence. (Round sensibly.)

2   Shapes A, B, and C have equal area. Arrange the shapes in order of *decreasing* perimeter.

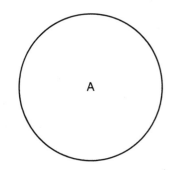
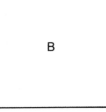
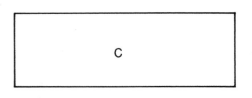

3   A 2-liter container for Top Lick ice cream currently has dimensions of 16 cm × 16 cm × 8 cm. It is roughly in the shape of a cuboid.

    a An industrial designer suggests that it would be cheaper to make the container in the shape of a cylinder. Explain the reasoning behind this.

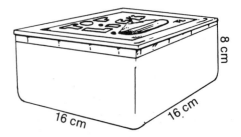

b i Use the formula $V = 2\pi r^3$ to find the radius of the cylinder that minimizes the surface area of the container. (The area of the lid is included.)

   ii What is the height of the cylindrical container?

c Another designer suggests that a container in the shape of a cube would be best. Is she correct? Explain.

d Suggest reasons why the designers at Top Lick probably prefer their current container.

e Which of the two containers, the current 2-liter container or the cylindrical design, would allow the ice cream to freeze more quickly? Explain your answer.

4 A 10-liter plastic bucket in the shape of an open cylinder is designed so that the amount of plastic used is minimal. For minimum surface area, the volume can be determined from $V = \pi r^3$.

a Find the radius of the bucket. (Round sensibly.)

b Find the height of the bucket. (Round sensibly.)

c A manufacturer uses $h = 2r$ and $V = 2\pi r^3$ to produce 10-liter buckets.
   i Find r and h for such buckets.
   ii Find the surface area of such a bucket, using the formula $S = \pi r^2 + 2\pi rh$.
   iii Show that for manufacturers who produce buckets with a minimal surface area, there is a saving of about 5%.

5 It is often recommended that teapots be roughly spherical in shape. Explain the reasoning behind this.

CHAPTER TWO

PATTERNS

TEACHING NOTES

Patterns in number sequences frequently implicate some underlying functional relationship. We can use two-column tables to highlight the patterns as we systematically list problem outcomes. In the first column we keep track of the step $(0, 1, 2, ..., n)$, and in the second column we list the outcome at each step. A second type of pattern involving symmetric sequences of numbers emerges in two-player games with counters, enabling the complete analysis of winning strategies for each different game.

Investigation One • Patterns

By calculating the number of ancestors in a family, students discover how the theoretical solution (i.e., number of ancestors $= 2^0 + 2^1 + 2^2 + ... + 2^n$) compares to actual population demographics when, for large populations, distant relatives may unknowingly marry. They also see how the Fibonacci sequence (1, 1, 2, 3, 5, 8, 13, ...) can be used to describe the growth in bee and rabbit populations. Other pattern problems explored in this section include the classic Tower of Brahma problem (where the minimum number of moves for n discs is $2^n - 1$) and the challenge of finding the maximum number of regions formed by connecting n points on a circle — not, as it seems, 2^{n-1}, but rather a complicated fourth degree polynomial:

$$\frac{1}{24}(n^4 - 6n^3 + 23n^2 - 18n + 24)$$

This series of problems introduces students to finding a pattern in the sequential differences in two-column tables in order to extend a table without knowing the underlying function. Students also investigate Pick's theorem ($A = \frac{1}{2}b + i - 1$) through the systematic exploration of the number of trees in orchards of various shapes. In an *On Your Own* investigation, students explore independently a more general but lesser known form of Pick's theorem ($A = \frac{1}{2}b + i + n - 1$), where n is the number of *holes* in the region.

Investigation Two • Game Strategies

Students explore a number of two-player games with counters, sometimes called "Nim" games, that can be analyzed using symmetry. They discover that in many cases they can specify a strategy that enables them to accurately predict the winner simply by knowing who moves first. For example, by working backwards we can analyze the game Force-to-21 (starting at 1, two players take turns increasing the total by 1 or 2 until the loser is forced to say 21). To win, you must force your opponent to say 18; then you will in turn increase the total to 20 (adding 2), thereby forcing your opponent to 21 on the next move. Similarly, you must force your opponent to say 15, 12, 9, 6, and 3. The player who starts can force the second player to say 3, and therefore all multiples of 3, by adding 1 when the second player adds 2 and adding 2 when the second player adds 1. Through investigation, students find they can use this type of symmetric response (that is, alternating response types with the opponent) to develop a winning strategy for many Nim-type games.

Investigation One

Patterns

1 Tom Brown's family tree looks like this.

a i How many grandparents does Tom have?

ii How many great-grandparents does he have?

b Tom wonders how far back he had a million living ancestors. He prepares a table.

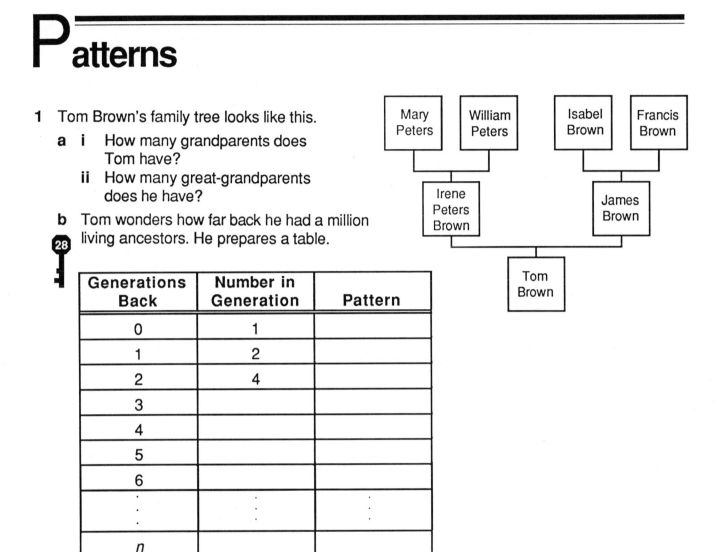

Generations Back	Number in Generation	Pattern
0	1	
1	2	
2	4	
3		
4		
5		
6		
⋮	⋮	⋮
n		

i Complete the table.

ii Find out how many generations back Tom had 1 000 000 ancestors. (Use a calculator.)

c Tom assumes that a new generation is born every 25 years. Work out approximately when 10 000 000 ancestors of Tom were alive.

d Suppose Tom's parents are *second cousins*. That is, Irene and James have a pair of great-grandparents in common. Extend the family tree to show that when $n = 4$, the number of Tom's ancestors is 14, *not* 16 as predicted in the table. (n = number of generations back)

e Tom's ancestors come from Britain and the population there did not reach 10 000 000 until well into the 19th century. Explain why the method you used in **b** and **c** must break down for large n. (Problem **d** contains an important clue.)

2 As part of her science studies, Rosemary learns that the life cycle of bees is quite different from that of other insects.

Male bees (drones) hatch from unfertilized eggs, and so have a mother but no father. Female bees hatch from fertilized eggs.

Rosemary begins a family tree of a male bee.

a Copy and extend the family tree to the fifth generation back.

b i Complete the table.

 ii Use patterns in the table to find out how many bees were in the twelfth generation back.

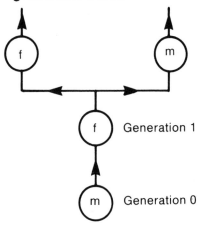

Generations Back	Number in Generation
0	1
1	1
2	2
3	
4	
5	
6	
7	

*O*N YOUR OWN

A male-female pair of one-month-old rabbits is released on a rabbit-free island. At one month old, they are too young to have offspring. Suppose that at the beginning of the third month of life and the beginning of every month thereafter, a pair of rabbits produce another male-female pair.

1 Find how many pairs of rabbits are on the island at the end of each month of a 12-month period. (Assume that none die.)

2 The sequence of numbers in problem **1** is called the *Fibonacci* sequence. Find out how musical scales are related to the Fibonacci sequence.

3 According to an ancient Hindu legend, Brahma placed
64 gold disks, one on top of the other, in the Tower of Brahma.
The disks, each a different size, were stacked in order with
the largest at the bottom and the smallest at the top.

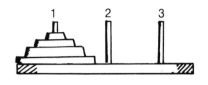

Priests were told to transfer the disks from one pile to another (via an
intermediary pile if necessary) so that at no stage would a larger disk be placed
on top of a smaller disk. The legend said that when the work was complete, the
world would end.

Luke decided to investigate this legend, so he made himself a simple model of the
Tower of Brahma (sometimes called the Tower of Hanoi). He simplified the
problem by first starting with one disk, then two, then three, and so on.

a Follow Luke's moves on a Tower of Brahma for two, three, and four disks. In
the tables, each column represents one of the three stacks, and each row
represents the position of each disk on that move.

one disk		
1	**2**	**3**
a		
		a

two disks		
1	**2**	**3**
ab		
a	b	
	b	a
		ab

three disks		
1	**2**	**3**
abc		
ab		c
a	b	c
a	bc	
	bc	a
c	b	a
c		ab
		abc

four disks		
1	**2**	**3**
abcd		
abc	d	
ab	d	c
ab		cd
a	b	cd
ad	b	c
ad	bc	
a	bcd	
	bcd	a
	bc	ad

b Complete the table for four disks, doing the moves on
a Tower of Brahma. Look for symmetry in the table.

c Complete this table.

Number of Disks	Minimum Number of Moves	Pattern
1	1	
2	3	
3	7	
4		
5		
6		
. . .	. . .	. . .
n		$2^{\square} - \square$

d **i** Find the minimum number of moves required to move 64 disks.

   ii Suppose it takes one second to move one disk. Is the legend's prediction regarding the end of the world reasonable? Explain your answer.

e Luke thinks he has a quick way to solve this problem. He knows that for 3 disks, 7 moves are needed. He reasons that the top 3 disks of a 4-disk tower require 7 moves to a temporary position. The fourth disk can then be transferred to its final position in a single move, and the 3 disks waiting in the intermediary position require 7 additional moves to reach their final position on top of the largest disk. The 4-disk tower therefore requires 7 + 1 + 7 = 15 moves.

   i Is Luke's reasoning correct?

   ii Use Luke's reasoning to calculate the minimum number of moves required for a 7-disk tower.

4 Amy challenges George to predict the maximum number of regions formed when 8 points on a circle are connected to each other. George finds it difficult to count regions when there are more than 5 points, so he solves a set of simpler problems using up to 5 points and then looks for a pattern.

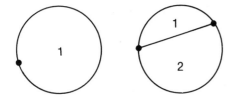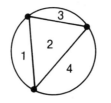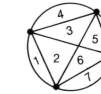

Number of Points	Number of Regions
1	1
2	2
3	4
4	
5	

a Complete George's table.

b **i** Predict what George will say for the number of regions for 6 points.

   ii Check this prediction by drawing a circle with 6 points and counting the regions.

   iii Is the prediction in problem **b i** correct?

c Amy used the following table to find the number of regions
for 7 and 8 points.

Number of Points	Number of Regions	First Difference	Second Difference	Third Difference
1	1			
2	2	1	1	
3	4	2	2	1
4	8	4	4	2
5	16	8	7	3
6	31	15		
7				
8				

i   Complete the table.
ii Can Amy be certain that she is correct?

5 Department of Agriculture officials want to help fruit growers quickly work
out the area of their orchards so that they can apply the correct amounts
of fertilizer.

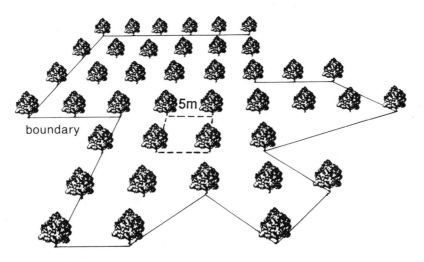

The diagram shows Chris's orchard. Trees are in rows and at the corners
of squares 5 m × 5 m. Helen, who is the department's mathematician,
notices that in Chris's orchard, trees are either on the boundary line or
inside the boundary.

Helen uses dot paper to investigate a variety of simple orchards and records each area (A) in a table.

a Find the areas of the simple orchards shown, plus some of your own design, and enter your results in the table below.

21

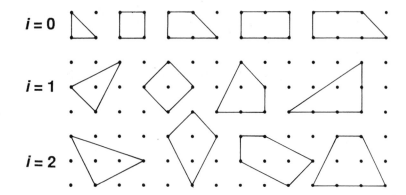

$i = 0$

$i = 1$

$i = 2$

Trees on Boundary (b)

		0	1	2	3	4	5	6	7
	0				$\frac{1}{2}$	1	$1\frac{1}{2}$		
Trees	1				$1\frac{1}{2}$				
inside	2								
Boundary	3								
(i)	4								
	5								

b i Complete the table by observing any patterns.
  ii Why is part of the table shaded?

c Helen writes the results for $i = 0$ in another table, shown at right. (A = area)

31
  i Complete the table.
  ii Complete the formula
  $A = \frac{1}{2}\,\square - 1.$

d Repeat **c** for the following values of i. Look for a developing pattern.
  i   1
  ii 2
  iii 3
  iv 4

b	A	Pattern
3	$\frac{1}{2}$	$\frac{1}{2} \times 3 - 1$
4	1	$\frac{1}{2} \times 4 - 1$
5	$1\frac{1}{2}$	
6		
7		
$\vdots$	$\vdots$	$\vdots$
b		$\frac{1}{2}\square - 1$

e i   Use your answers from **d** to help you complete the next table and
formula, $A = \square\, b + \triangle - 1$.

i	Formula for A	Pattern
0	$A = \frac{1}{2}b - 1$	$A = \frac{1}{2}b + 0 - 1$
1	$A = \frac{1}{2}b$	$A = \frac{1}{2}b + 1 - 1$
2	$A = \frac{1}{2}b + 1$	$A = \frac{1}{2}b + 2 - 1$
3		
4		
5		
$\vdots$		
i		$A = \square\, b + \triangle - 1$

ii   Check that for Chris's orchard, $b = 24$ and $i = 17$. Then show that
his orchard has an area of 0.07 hectare. (A hectare is the metric
unit for the area of a square 100 m on a side. How many football
fields equal about 1 hectare?)

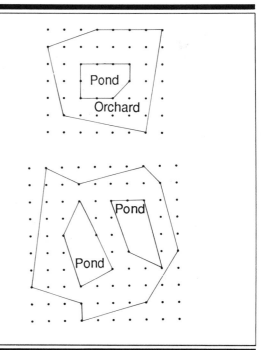

ON YOUR OWN

Helen uses the methods in problem **5**
to find a formula for the area of an
orchard with one pond in the middle.

1   Follow those same methods to find a
formula for the area involving b, the
number of boundary trees (which
includes the trees on the boundary
of the pond), and i, the number of
trees inside the boundaries.

2   Repeat problem **1** for orchards with
a 2 ponds.   **b** 3 ponds.

3   Find a formula for the area when
there are n ponds.

6 The number 7 is the sum of consecutive whole numbers because 7 = 3 + 4. So is the number 10, because 10 = 1 + 2 + 3 + 4. (For this problem, do not use zero as a whole number.)

a Show that 8 is *not* the sum of consecutive whole numbers.

b **i** Is 29 the sum of two consecutive whole numbers?
ii Investigate which numbers are the sum of two consecutive whole numbers. Look for a pattern.

c Find patterns to predict which numbers are the sum of the following:
i three consecutive whole numbers.
ii four consecutive whole numbers.
iii five consecutive whole numbers.
iv six consecutive whole numbers.

d By summarizing your results in **b** and **c**, find a simple rule to predict which numbers are, or are not, the sum of consecutive whole numbers.

e Test to see whether or not each of the following is the sum of consecutive whole numbers.
i 127
ii 128
iii 254
iv 256
v 1024

7 The number 24 is the sum of consecutive *odd* numbers because 24 = 3 + 5 + 7 + 9.

a Investigate which numbers are the sum of consecutive odd numbers.

b The number 18 is the sum of consecutive *even* numbers because 18 = 4 + 6 + 8. Investigate which numbers are the sum of consecutive even numbers.

c Find a simple rule to test whether a number is neither the sum of consecutive odd numbers nor the sum of consecutive even numbers.

d Test the following numbers against your rule.
i 17
ii 27
iii 49
iv 51
v 53

8 In Janine's class of 28 students, everyone buys one raffle ticket. The tickets are numbered from 1 through 28 with the number printed in blue on one side and in red on the other side. Prize winners are found according to the rules shown at right.

a Prepare tickets like the ones described, making one for every member of your class. Distribute the tickets randomly.

b Run through the rules carefully. You may have to do a rerun, as someone usually fails to follow instructions.

RULES FOR THE RAFFLE

- Students will hold their tickets with the red number facing up.
- Students must then follow this sequence of instructions:

  Step 1: Flip your ticket over if it is a multiple of 1.

  Step 2: Flip your ticket over if it is a multiple of 2.

  Step 3: Flip your ticket over if it is a multiple of 3.

  Step 4: Continue flipping in this way for multiples of 4, 5, and so on, up to the total number in the class.

- Prize winners are those left with blue numbers facing up at the completion of the flipping.

---

c i What are the winning tickets in your class?
   ii In Janine's class, what would the winning tickets be?

d Describe the pattern in the winning numbers.

e Suppose that everyone in your school was given a ticket like this at a school assembly.
   i Write down your estimate of the total number of tickets needed for your school.
   ii Write down the winning numbers at your school.

f Janine wants to understand why the pattern of winning numbers works.
   i Complete the table.
   ii Show why the rule for determining a winning ticket always works.

Ticket Number	Flip On	Number of Flips	Winner/Loser
1	1	1	winner
2	1, 2	2	loser
3	1, 3	2	
4	1, 2, 4	3	
5	1, 5	2	
6	1, 2, 3, 6	4	
7			
8			
9			
10			

Investigation Two

Game Strategies

It is important to play the games in this investigation in order to find the winning strategies.

1 Paul challenges Kathy to a game of skill called Take-Away.

Choose a partner in your class and be ready to play Take-Away.

a Suppose one of you takes all of pile A or pile B as your first move. Why is this a losing strategy?

b Paul and Kathy realize it will be hard to find a winning strategy with 8 and 11 counters, so first they solve a set of simpler problems. The number of counters in each pile is listed under A and B in the table. Assume Paul starts each game. Play the games up to 8 and 11 counters and extend the table to record your results. Try to be systematic.

c i Show by experiment that if A = 2 and B = 2, Kathy can *always* force a win.
  ii Then show that if A = 7 and B = 2, Paul can always win.

d Who can always force a win if A = 3 and B = 3?

e Continue to play Take-Away games with various pairs of A and B until you discover a simple winning strategy.

f Challenge other members of the class who think they have a winning strategy to play Take-Away with you.

g Explain why the following rules work when Paul starts:

  • If A ≠ B, Paul can force a win.

  • If A = B, Kathy can force a win.

RULES FOR TAKE-AWAY

• Each player in turn removes any number of counters (at least 1) from *one* of the piles (A or B, but *not* both at once).

• The winner is the player who takes the last counter or group of counters.

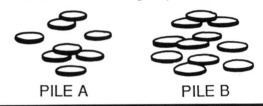

PILE A   PILE B

Pile A	Pile B	First Move by Paul	Winner
1	1	1 from A	Kathy
1	1	1 from B	Kathy
2	1	1 from B	Kathy
2	1	2 from A	
2	1	1 from A	
2	2	2 from A	Kathy
2	2	2 from B	
.	.		
.	.		
.	.		

ON YOUR OWN

Play Take-Away using three piles of counters instead of two. Devise a winning strategy.

2 In Knock Down, a bowling-type game, a ball is rolled at wooden pins standing side by side.

The ball is big enough to knock down either one single pin or two pins standing side by side. Players alternately roll a ball, and the player who knocks over the last pin (or pair of pins) is the winner. Assume you can always hit the desired pins.

a Using nine counters to simulate Knock Down, play the game with another person.

b Devise a winning strategy if you have the first throw. (Hint: compare this problem with the Take-Away game in problem **1**.)

c Jordan observes that the winning strategy involves maintaining symmetry among the wooden pins. Explain what he means.

3 a Choose an opponent to play Cover Up using these rules. The game board can be any size. A 5 × 3 game board is shown as an illustration.

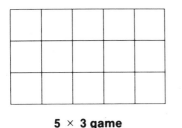

5 × 3 game

RULES FOR COVER UP

- Players take alternate turns at adding 1 or 2 counters to the board.
- Two counters added in the same turn must be on adjacent squares—that is, squares that share one side.

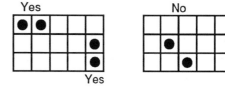

- The winner is the player who makes the last move.

b To find a winning strategy for Cover Up, play games on grids of the sizes shown in the table below. Show that the entries in the table are correct. Assume that the second player knows a winning strategy and is just waiting for an error by the first player to apply it.

Grid Size	1st Move ●	2nd Move ✕	3rd Move ●	Winning Player
1 x 1	[●]	(none)	(none)	first
2 x 1	[● ●]	(none)	(none)	first
3 x 1	[_ ● _]	[✕ ● _]	[✕ ● ●]	first
3 x 1	[● _ _]	[● ✕ ✕]	(none)	second
4 x 1	[● _ _ _]	[● _ ✕ _]	[● ● ✕ _]	second
4 x 1	[_ ● _ _]	[_ ● _ ✕]	[● ● _ ✕]	second
4 x 1	[_ ● ● _]	[_ ● ● ✕]	[● ● ● ✕]	first
4 x 1	[● ● _ _]	[● ● ✕ ✕]	(none)	second
5 x 1	[● _ _ _ _]	[● _ ✕ ✕ _]	[● _ ✕ ✕ ●]	
5 x 1	[_ ● _ _ _]	[_ ● _ ✕ ✕]	[● ● _ ✕ ✕]	
5 x 1	[_ _ ● _ _]	[_ _ ● _ ✕]	[_ ● ● _ ✕]	
⋮	⋮	⋮	⋮	

c The first player can always win on a $n \times 1$ (or $1 \times n$) grid. What is the winning strategy? Does it involve symmetry?

d Find winning strategies by playing Cover Up games on grids of the following sizes, stating which player must win.

   i 2×2 **ii** 2×3 **iii** 2×4 **iv** 2×5 **v** 2×6

e Repeat **d** for the following:

   i 3×3 **iii** 3×5

   ii 3×4 **iv** 3×6

f **i** Summarize the winners from **b**, **d**, and **e** in the table at right.

   ii Suppose both players know the winning strategy. State the strategy for any size grid and say which person will win.

Winners for Various Grid Sizes

	1	2	3	4	5	6
1	1st	1st	1st			
2	1st	2nd				
3	1st					
4	1st					
5						
6						

35

ONYOUROWN

In this game the object is to force your opponent's counters to his or her end of the board, thereby preventing further moves. Devise a winning strategy for Push Back, following the given rules.

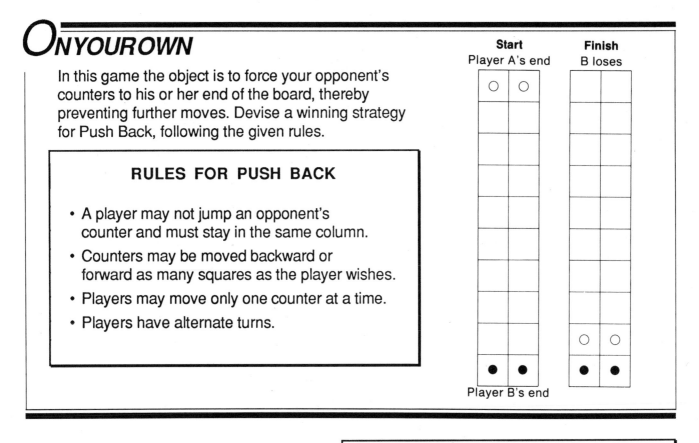

Start Player A's end

Finish B loses

Player B's end

RULES FOR PUSH BACK

- A player may not jump an opponent's counter and must stay in the same column.
- Counters may be moved backward or forward as many squares as the player wishes.
- Players may move only one counter at a time.
- Players have alternate turns.

4 Simone and Anthony played the game Factor Subtractor.

a The table below shows how they played the first game.
  i Who wins this game? Explain your answer.

RULES FOR FACTOR SUBTRACTOR
- Players choose any number to start the game.
- Each player in turn subtracts any factor of the number (except the number itself) left by the opponent.
- The winner is the last player who can perform such a subtraction.

Player	Factor Subtracted	Total After Subtraction
Start	—	12
Anthony	2	10
Simone	5	5
Anthony	1	4
Simone	2	2
Anthony	1	1
⋮	⋮	⋮

b Play Factor Subtractor with a partner. Will you win or lose if you are left with the following number?
  i 2
  ii 3
  Explain your answer in each case.

c Suppose you are left with the number 4.
  i How will you ensure a win?
  ii How will you ensure a loss?

d To find a winning strategy for Factor Subtractor, Simone makes a table to investigate systematically all possible subtractions near the end of a game.

Number Left for Simone	Factor Subtracted	Number Left for Anthony	Winner
2	1	1	Simone
3	1	2	
4	2	2	
4	1	3	
5	1		
6	3		
6	2		
6	1		
8	4		
8	2		
8	1		
9	3		
9	1		
10	5		
10	2		
10	1		

i Complete the table and look for a winning strategy.

ii Suppose Simone is left with the number 12. Which of the factors (1, 2, 3, 4, or 6) should she subtract from 12? Explain your answer.

e Suppose the winner is the last player who *cannot* perform a subtraction. What is a winning strategy now?

ON YOUR OWN

In Count Down, eight counters are placed at the corners of an octagon. The game is for two players with the following rules. Devise a winning strategy for this game if it is played on *any* regular polygon.

RULES FOR COUNT DOWN

- A player must remove one or two counters. If two are removed, they must be from adjacent positions.
- Players have alternate turns.
- The last player to move wins.

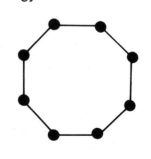

5   The game of Force Out has these
    rules for two players.

    For example, if the starting number
    is 11 and Player A starts, we might
    have the following:

Player	Number Subtracted	Current Total
Start	—	11
A	2	9
B	1	8
A	2	6
B	1	5
A	2	3
B	2	1
A	1	0

RULES FOR FORCE OUT

- Any whole number is selected as the beginning total.
- Each player must take away 1 or 2 to create a current total.
- Players have alternate turns.
- The player who makes the current total zero is forced out and loses the game.

PLAYER A IS FORCED TO ZERO AND LOSES.

a   Select a partner and play to confirm that the following table is correct.
    Assume A and B are expert players who will not make errors, and A
    always starts. Complete the table, extending it to 11.

Beginning Total	First Number Subtracted by A	Eventual Winner Must Be . . .
1	1	B
2	1	A
2	2	B
3	1	B
3	2	A
4	1	B
4		B
5		
.	.	.
.	.	.
.	.	.

b   Player A knows that if she wants to win, she must force the total left
    after her turn to be certain numbers; otherwise she will lose. What are
    these numbers? What is the pattern?

c   Who will win with the following beginning totals? Remember: Player A
    starts first.
    i 36   **ii** 37   **iii** 38   **iv** 97   **v** 98

6 a Suppose Force Out is played using 1, 2, or 3 as the numbers that can be subtracted. Go through a process similar to that in problem **5** to find a winning strategy.

b Extend your work in **a** to find the winning strategy when the following are the numbers that may be subtracted.
   i 1, 2, 3, or 4
   ii 1, 2, 3, 4, or 5
   iii 1, 2, 3, 4, 5, or 6

c Give the winning strategy if the numbers that can be subtracted are 1, 2, 3, 4, ..., *n*. Find a pattern for subtracting up to any number *n*.

7 Find a winning strategy for Force Out in which the numbers 1, 2, 3, ..., 10 may be subtracted and the winner is the first to create a new total of zero.

8 Laura and Elizabeth play the game WInner Takes All.

RULES FOR WINNER TAKES ALL

• The first player selects any reasonably large number.

• The two players alternately subtract any number that is not greater than twice the number subtracted by the opponent on the previous play. (The first number must be less than the starting number.)

• The winner is the player who can *take all*—that is, leave nothing.

---

a Laura selects 26 to start and Elizabeth subtracts 9.
   i Explain why Laura can win easily.
   ii Explain why it would have been wiser for Elizabeth to have subtracted 8 or less.
   iii As she gains experience, Elizabeth realizes that she should never subtract one-third or more of the total left to her. Explain Elizabeth's reasoning.
b **i** Near the end of a game, Laura subtracts 1 to leave Elizabeth with 3. Explain why Laura *must* win.
   ii In another game, Elizabeth subtracts 1 to leave Laura with 5. Show that with skillful playing, Elizabeth can always win.

---

c The following table shows how Laura and Elizabeth play a game of Winner Takes All. The starting total is 43 and Laura has first turn.

| | Laura's Turn | | Elizabeth's Turn | |
Round	Number Taken	Number Left	Number Taken	Number Left
0	—	43	—	43
1	9	34	11	23
2	2	21	4	17
3	4	13	4	9
4	1	8	2	6
5	1	5	1	4
6	1	3	1	2
7	2	0		

The Fibonacci sequence is 1, 1, 2, 3, 5, 8, 13, 21 ...

Laura always leaves Elizabeth with a Fibonacci number.

i Explain Laura's reasoning.

ii Will Laura's strategy always work?

d Elizabeth notices Laura's strategy but also recalls the following:

All non-Fibonacci numbers can be written as the sum of two or more nonconsecutive Fibonacci numbers.

So $17 = 13 + 3 + 1$.

If Elizabeth is left with 17, she subtracts 1 (the smallest Fibonacci number in the sum $17 = 13 + 3 + 1$).

i Explain how this decision will ensure that Elizabeth can leave her opponent with the Fibonacci number 13.

ii Use Elizabeth's strategy to play the game. Is it always successful?

CHECK-UP

1 Kyle has seven bills in his wallet, including a $1, $2, $5, $10, $20, $50, and $100 bill. He wants to find out how many different amounts he can make with the seven bills.

Kyle simplifies the problem by first calculating the different amounts possible using only 1 bill ($1), then 2 bills ($1, $2), and so on.

a Complete the table. Look for patterns.

Different Bills Used	Total Amounts Possible ($)	Total No. of Amounts
$1	1	1
$1, $2	1, 2, 3	3
$1, $2, $5	1, 2, 3, 5, 6, 7, 8	7
$1, $2, $5, $10	1, 2, 3, 5, 6, 7, 8, 10, 11, 12 ...	
$1, $2, $5, $10, $20		
$1, $2, $5, $10, $20, $50		
$1, $2, $5, $10, $20, $50, $100		

b Suppose Kyle has the same seven bills plus five coins, worth 1¢, 5¢, 10¢, 25¢, and 50¢. How many amounts can he make now?

2 The North-East game is played with a partner, using a grid of any size for the board. Shown here is a 5 × 3 game board.

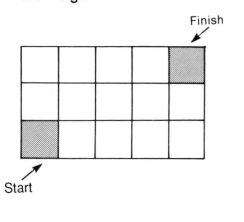

Finish

Start

RULES FOR NORTH-EAST

• Take turns placing counters on the board, starting in the square at the bottom left-hand corner.

• If your partner places a counter in the square marked O, you must place your counter in one of the three squares indicated with arrows. That is, thinking of the points on a compass, you must either move one square north, one square east, or one square northeast.

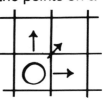

• The winner is the first to reach the square at the top right-hand corner.

a A 2 × 2 grid is the simplest board for North-East. The second player can always win. Explain how.

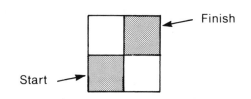

b On each grid in the table, mark an X to show the move that the second player must make to ensure a win.

c On the 3 × 3 grid, show the strategy that the first player should use to ensure a win.

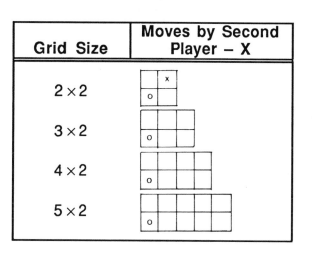

Grid Size	Moves by Second Player – X
2 × 2	
3 × 2	
4 × 2	
5 × 2	

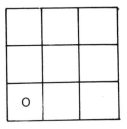

d Find winning strategies for playing North-East with boards of the following grid sizes. Indicate who will win in each case.
  i 4 × 3   **ii** 5 × 3   **iii** 6 × 3   **iv** 7 × 3

e Extend your work in **d** for the following grid sizes.
  i 4 × 4   **ii** 5 × 4   **iii** 6 × 4   **iv** 7 × 4

f i Use your results from **d** and **e** as you complete this summary table.

Winners for Various Grid Sizes

	Grid Width					
	2	**3**	**4**	**5**	**6**	**7**
2	2nd	2nd	2nd	2nd	2nd	2nd
3	2nd	1st				
4	2nd					
5	2nd					
6	2nd					
7	2nd					

(Grid Length — vertical label on left)

  ii State the winning strategy for playing North-East with any size grid. Indicate which squares are "winning" squares.

CHAPTER THREE

Operations Research

TEACHING NOTES

Operations research involves the application of scientific principles to real-world problems. We can sometimes use geometric and number patterns to unravel the underlying structure of the problem and predict results. Often, we can construct and graph a table of observations, and extrapolate for additional cases the pattern we observe. The procedure assumes that the relationship expressed is proportional and therefore can be sensibly extended. In any given case, we can test several extrapolated points to see if this assumption is reasonable.

Investigation One • Guarding the Gallery

A point exists on any pentagon, concave or convex, that can be connected with a straight line to any other point inside the figure without crossing an edge. Students use this geometric feature to explore the installation of security cameras in various irregularly shaped rooms (shaped as a triangle, quadrilateral, pentagon, hexagon, and so forth). They find that separating the room into the minimum number of pentagons, quadrilaterals, and triangles provides a systematic way to predict how many security cameras will be needed to "sweep" the entire floor space, and further discover that the maximum number of cameras needed equals the number of walls ÷ 3 (ignoring the decimal fraction).

Investigation Two • Forecasting

Forecasting involves the prediction of an event based on prior experience. For example, a simple hand-held calculator cost about $500 in 1973. By graphing the cost of similar calculators for subsequent years, you might predict that the cost would be $0 in 1985. Of course, the cost can never be zero because the packaging and marketing costs remain about constant, but the example does forecast the declining cost of the processing chip, which contributed perhaps 99% of the manufacturing cost of the calculator in 1973 and only 1% in 1985. Students try forecasting record track times, book inventories, stock prices, and sales figures in this section. You may want to discuss with the students the possible problems with the reliability of forecasts when certain assumptions are violated (for example, we know that human endurance is physically limited) and when related conditions change (for example, stock prices will be affected by political, economic, and psychological factors).

Investigation Three • Traveling Sales Rep Problem

Calculating the number of different ways to travel among fully interconnected cities (meaning that every city is directly connected to every other city) is equivalent to the number of permutations of the city names; that is, the number of routes equals $(n-1)!$. Students work with tree diagrams to systematically list all possible routes for a given network. A table of results is constructed and the factorial pattern is defined, enabling students to predict results for a larger number of cities. For an interesting extension, have students try solving this problem for a network in which some cities are *not* connected to all other cities.

Investigation Four • Mazes and Caving

Students explore the "left-hand-traversal" rule for getting through a maze. They find that if the maze is connected (that is, there is only one maze—not two or more intertwined, disconnected mazes), following this rule results in the traversal of the entire maze exactly twice, eventually leading to an exit. Students also investigate an alternative set of rules for traversing a cave with three-dimensional passages.

Investigation One

Guarding the Gallery

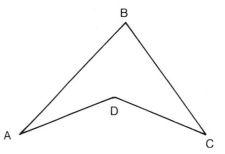

1 A security firm is hired to watch over the paintings at a special art gallery exhibition. The firm installs a closed-circuit TV (CCTV) system to guard the gallery. Cameras are to be installed *only* at corners of the room.

The gallery is in the shape of a concave quadrilateral like the one shown here. The operations director of the security firm believes that just one camera is sufficient to guard the gallery.

a i Show where the camera can be stationed. Give all solutions.
ii Is it possible to design a quadrilateral gallery that needs two cameras?

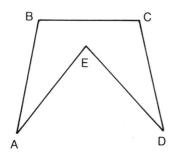

b i How many cameras are needed for this pentagonal gallery?
ii Where should the camera(s) be stationed?
iii Is it possible to design a pentagonal gallery that needs two or more cameras?

c The security firm is asked to guard a hexagonal gallery. The operations director advises that two cameras may be required.
i Design a hexagonal gallery that requires two cameras.
ii Exchange your design with a partner to check that two cameras are needed.

2 The operations director of the security firm wants to know at which corners they should install cameras to guard this hexagonal gallery. (From problem **1b**, we know that one camera is sufficient to guard any pentagonal gallery.)

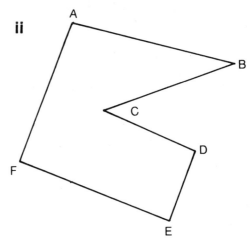

a Can this gallery be guarded with just one camera? Check all possibilities.

b Copy the diagram of the gallery and imagine that a wall, represented by a line CE, is added to create two smaller galleries, ABCEF and CDE.
   i Where should one camera be placed to guard the pentagonal gallery ABCEF?
   ii Where should one camera be placed to guard the triangular gallery CDE?

c Find all possible pairs of camera locations to guard ABCDEF by installing the following imaginary walls.
   i CE
   ii FB
   iii BE
   iv AB extended to meet the wall FE
   v CB extended to meet the wall FE
   vi DE extended to meet the wall BC
   vii FE extended to meet the wall CD

   Which pairs of cameras are best? Explain why.

d Find all camera locations to guard the four galleries below with the fewest cameras possible. In each case indicate which camera positions are best and explain why they are the best.

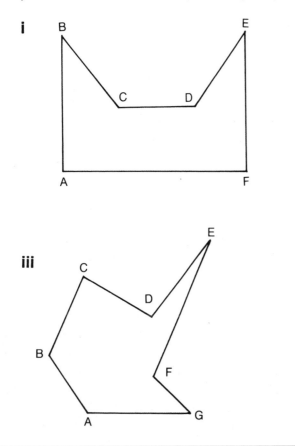

i

ii

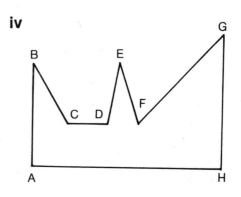

iii

iv

e i Complete the table at the right.

ii The operations director uses the completed table to deduce that an octagon will require no more than two cameras. Explain this reasoning.

Gallery Shape	Imaginary Wall Installed to Form
hexagon	pentagon + triangle
heptagon	pentagon +
octagon	pentagon +

f Draw examples of 9-, 10-, 11-, and 12-sided figures to help you complete this table.

Number of Sides of Gallery	Number of Pentagons Possible	Shape Remaining	Number of Cameras for Worst Case
3	0	triangle	1
4	0	quadrilateral	1
5	1	—	1
6	1	triangle	2
7	1		
8	2		
9			
10			
11			
12			

g Design some odd-shaped galleries for **i, ii,** and **iii** below and show that the rule for calculating the number of cameras holds.

i 9-sided gallery   **ii** 10-sided gallery   **iii** 12-sided gallery

3 In this table, n is the number of walls in the gallery and c is the *minimum* number of cameras required, in the *worst* case, to guard the gallery.

a Complete the table. Use the table in problem **2f** to help.

b Find c for the following galleries, where n is the number of walls.

   i $n = 20$ **ii** $n = 48$ **iii** $n = 102$

c Write in words the rule for the number of cameras needed for an n-sided gallery.

d Draw polygons that show these statements are true.

   i A 13-sided gallery may need 4 cameras.

   ii A 15-sided gallery may need 5 cameras.

   iii A 21-sided gallery may need 7 cameras.

n	c
3	1
4	1
5	1
6	2
7	
8	
9	
10	
11	
12	

Investigation Two

Forecasting

1 This table shows world-record times for the mile run from 1954 to 1985 (rounded to the nearest second).

a Graph the data.

b Fit a curve or line to the data as best you can.

c Predict when the world record will be
   i   3 minutes 40 seconds.
   ii 3 minutes 10 seconds.
   Explain your answers carefully.

Date	Time
May 1954	3 min 59 s
June 1954	3 min 58 s
July 1957	3 min 57 s
August 1958	3 min 55 s
January 1962	3 min 54 s
July 1967	3 min 51 s
August 1975	3 min 49 s
August 1981	3 min 48 s
August 1981	3 min 47 s
July 1985	3 min 46 s

2 A publishing house estimates it will have to move to premises with more storage when sales reach $1.3 million per year. The table shows the company's sales history.

a Graph the data.

b Fit a curve or line to the data as best you can.

c Predict when the company will have to move.

Year	Sales ($)
1	801 000
2	914 000
3	996 000
4	1 096 000

3 Rosemary is interested in the stock market. She reads the paper and records the share price of Zodet Software each Monday.

Week	Sales Price ($)
0	13.41
1	13.42
2	13.60
3	13.58
4	13.70
5	13.68
6	13.70
7	13.80
8	13.82

a Graph her data.

b Predict what the share price will be
  i   in week 9.
  ii in week 12.
  iii in week 20.

c Comment on the reliability of your predictions.

ON YOUR OWN

Using the business section of a newspaper, record the share price for a particular company each Monday. Predict future share prices and compare your predictions with the actual prices as you get them.

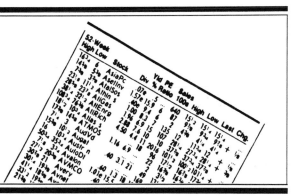

4 The Sunspecs Company manufactures sunglasses. The table shows company sales for four years.

Year	Sales (in thousands of dollars by quarters)			
	July–Sept	Oct–Dec	Jan–March	April–June
1986	7.2	2.4	5.1	7.0
1987	7.6	3.1	5.0	5.9
1988	8.8	4.1	6.8	7.4
1989	10.3	5.3	7.1	7.5

a What do you think explains the seasonal variation in sales?

b Graph the sales figures.

c Predict the sales figures for each quarter of 1990.

d How reliable do you expect your predictions to be?

Investigation Three

Traveling Sales Rep Problem

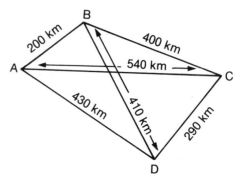

1 Angela is a traveling sales representative, or "sales rep," who lives in City A. She plans to visit customers in cities B, C, and D by plane and then return home. Angela wants to solve the Traveling Sales Rep problem—that is, she wants to find the route that will minimize the distance of her journey. She does not visit cities B, C, or D twice.

a Complete the tree diagram and the table.

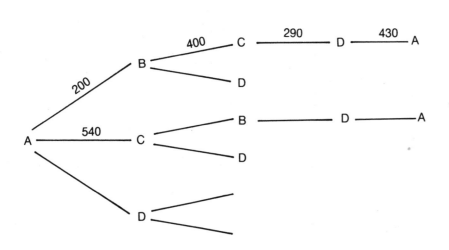

Route	Distance (km)
ABCDA	1320
ACBDA	

b Solve the Traveling Sales Rep problem for Angela's case.

c i Does route ABCDA = route ADCBA?
ii Ryan claims there are only three, not six, possible routes for the sales rep. Explain this reasoning.

2 a Solve the Traveling Sales Rep problem for this network. Home base is H.

b If the sales rep is based at G instead of H, does the solution change?

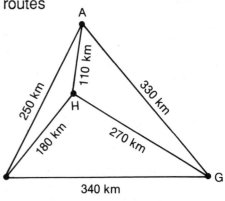

3 a Solve the Traveling Sales Rep problem for a person based at W.

    b Solve the problem for a person based at M.

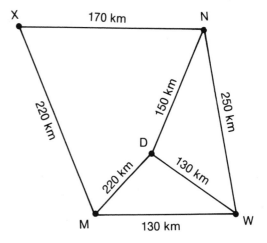

4 Solve the Traveling Sales Rep problem for this network. The sales rep is based at E.

5 Use the distance chart to solve the Traveling Sales Rep problem for this network.

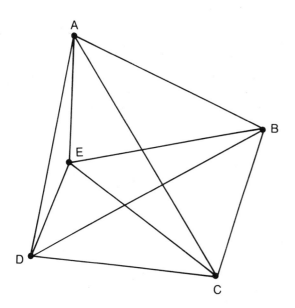

	B	C	D	E	
A	20	25	27	15	A
B		13	29	19	B
C			21	16	C
D				15	D

Distances (km)

a Prepare a tree diagram to help solve this problem. The sales rep is based at C. (Be careful: There are 24 routes!)

b Find the minimum distance for a trip to all the cities.

6 Now consider this network. The distances are shown in the chart.

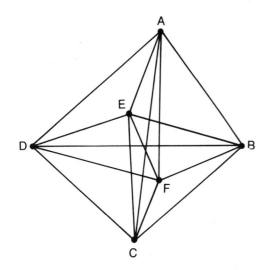

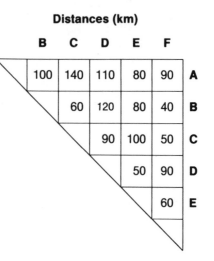

Distances (km)

	B	C	D	E	F	
	100	140	110	80	90	**A**
		60	120	80	40	**B**
			90	100	50	**C**
				50	90	**D**
					60	**E**

a Try to solve the Traveling Sales Rep problem for this network using a tree diagram. The sales representative is based at A.

b What difficulty do you encounter?

c On a block of wood, put nails at A, B, C, D, E, and F. (Alternatively, you could use a pegboard.) Make sure your network is a reasonably accurate scale representation of the network shown here.

   i Try various routes by stretching a rubber band around the nails or pegs.

   ii Find a good solution by using the rubber band.

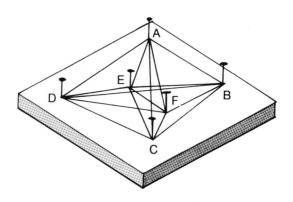

Oɴ YOUR OWN

1 Make up a Traveling Sales Rep problem for the area in which you live. Use at least eight points-of-call.

2 Use a board and nails or a pegboard to show the details of your problem.

3 Solve your Traveling Sales Rep problem.

7 This table, based on the Traveling Sales Rep problem, summarizes the possible number of routes involved in visiting each town once and returning home.

Number of Towns	Number of Routes	Pattern
3	2	$2! = 2 \times 1$
4	6	$3! = 3 \times 2 \times 1$
5	24	$4! = 4 \times 3 \times 2 \times 1$
6		
7		
8		
9		

a Complete the table. (Note that 2! is called "two factorial" and is calculated as shown in the Pattern column.)

b i How many routes are possible for 20 towns?
   ii Suppose a computer can work out the length of one million routes per second. How many years would the computer take to find the shortest route by inspecting every possibility?

c Is the tree diagram method for solving the Traveling Sales Rep problem useful when $n \geq 5$? (n = number of towns)

Investigation Four

Mazes and Caving

1 A visitor to a maze thinks he has dropped his wallet. He re-enters, planning to *traverse* (which means walk entirely through every segment of) the maze. An attendant gives him the following rule, called the "left-hand-traversal rule."

> **Put your left hand on the wall and walk, keeping your hand in contact with a wall at all times. This way you will traverse the maze.**

Investigate the truth of this rule for the maze shown here.

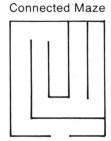

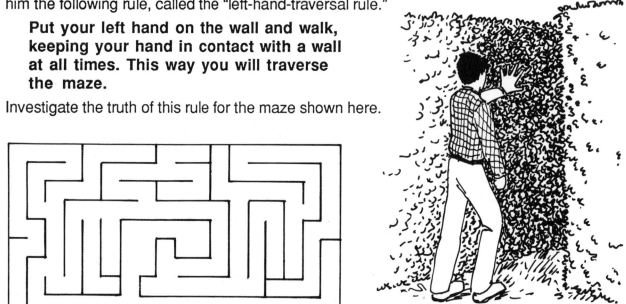

In/Out

2 a On graph paper, design a number of mazes with the entrance and exit at the same place. Make sure that each line is connected to another line in your maze, so that no part of the maze is disconnected from the rest. (See the examples of a connected and disconnected maze.)

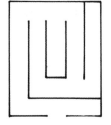

Connected Maze   Disconnected Maze

b Investigate whether the left-hand-traversal rule works for your connected mazes.

c Using the left-hand-traversal rule on your mazes, would a visitor cover every part of the maze exactly twice?

3   Sarah drops her credit card in a maze and notices this only after leaving the maze.
Unknown to Sarah, her card is at X.

On this maze, show how Sarah can use the left-hand-traversal rule to find her credit card.

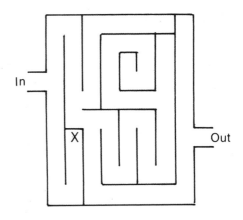

4   Repeat problem **2**, except this time make mazes with **separate** entrances and exits, like the one in problem **3**.

5   In an act of bravado, John foolishly leaves his caving group while underground. When the group returns to the surface, they realize John is missing and could be lying injured somewhere. There is no map of the caves.

    a   Would the left-hand-traversal rule guarantee they would find John in any cave system? Why or why not?

    b   If they do use the left-hand-traversal rule, what markers do they need to leave as they search?

6   Paramedics need to reach Eric, who has collapsed in this maze at point X. Will the left-hand-traversal rule allow the paramedics to reach him? Explain your answer.

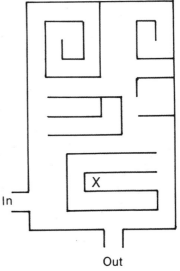

7   **a**   Repeat problem **2**, except this time use **disconnected** mazes.

    b   Reconsider your answer to problem **6** if necessary.

8   A mathematician provides the members of a caving club (sometimes called *spelunkers*) with the following rules to help them search an unmapped cave system in the event that a club member is lost.

RULES FOR SEARCHING A CAVE NETWORK

1 Your last move is to return to the cave entrance.

2 If you come to the end of a branch of the cave, turn around and go back. If you arrive at an exit, turn around and go back.

3 Clearly mark where you have walked, particularly the intersections (for example, leave a chalk mark each time you pass an intersection).

4 Use all routes exactly twice.

5 When you arrive at a new intersection, choose any route as your next move.

6 When you arrive at a used intersection, then:

   a if the route you walked has been used just once, immediately turn around and retrace that route.

   b if the route you just walked has been used twice, walk along any unused route available from that intersection. If no new routes are available, pick a route that has been used only once.

---

a Following the numbered arrows in these two diagrams of the same cave network, check that the rules have been correctly applied.

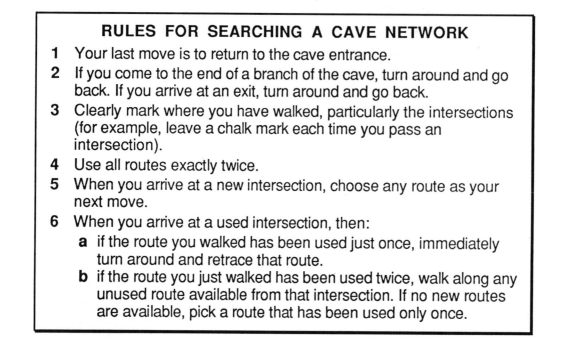

b Make four copies of this network and, by using the mathematician's rules, find four different ways of traversing the network.

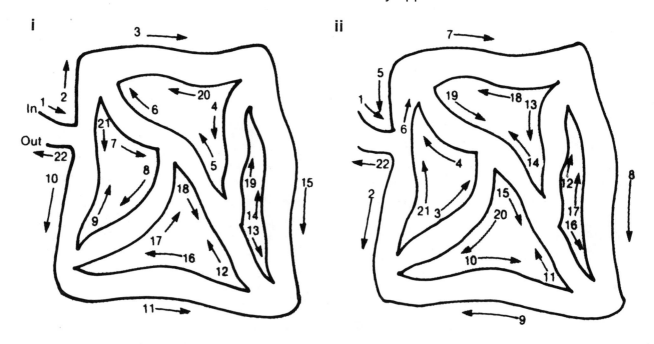

9 Peter knows that the left-hand-traversal rule will not always take him to all parts of the maze, but he thinks that it *will* get him in and out of any maze. Is Peter's generalization correct for this maze?

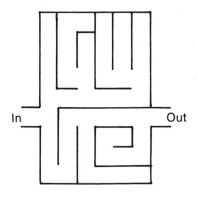

In   Out

CLASS INVESTIGATION

1 Can you design a cave system for which the mathematician's rules in problem **8** fail?

2 If you think you have such a design, get the rest of the class to check it.

ON YOUR OWN

1 Design your own mazes and check whether or not Peter's generalization in problem **9** is correct.

2 If Peter is correct, can you explain why?

CHECK-UP

1 Design a nine-sided art gallery that needs only three cameras to guard it.

2 Someone lies injured in this cave at point Y. Show how you could locate her and then get her out. Assume that no map is available.

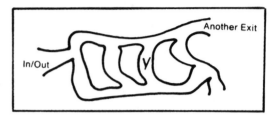

3 Solve the Traveling Sales Rep Problem for each network below. Assume that the sales rep starts at X in each case. (All distances are in kilometers.)

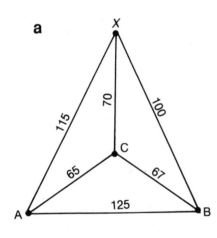

a

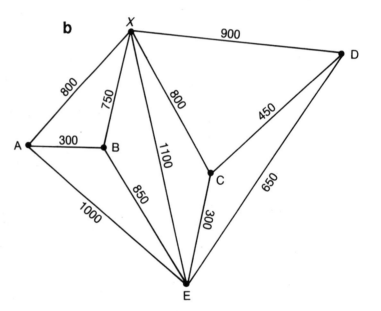

b

4 This table shows one company's market share of bicycle sales for six years.

a Graph the data.

b Predict what the company's market share will be
i in 1990.
ii in 1995.

How reliable are your predictions?

Year	Market Share
1984	31%
1985	32%
1986	26%
1987	25%
1988	20%
1989	20%

CHAPTER FOUR

PHOTOGRAPHY

TEACHING NOTES

With today's automatic cameras, taking photographs often seems as simple as pointing the camera and pressing a button, but in fact many variables affect the proper exposure of film, working together to produce pictures that are neither too dark, nor washed out, nor blurry. Several different sequences of numbers describe these variables. The photographer (or the camera's processor) must coordinate shutter speed (exposure time), f-stop, depth of field, and ASA film speed to achieve the desired effect. Because so many of the cameras sold now make all these adjustments automatically, students may not be familiar with the type of camera that is adjusted manually. If possible, have one available in the classroom for their reference during these investigations.

Investigation One • Shutter Times and f-stops

In this section students explore how the length of time the shutter remains open and how wide it is open work together in the proper exposure of film, discovering the relationship between shutter speed and aperture size (f-stop). They find that the shutter exposure scale is calibrated so that the photographer can sequentially double the time the lens remains open in order to compensate for proportional increments in the size of the aperture. The f-stop scale is a measure of the area of the aperture through which light passes. Increasing the f-stop one increment, or *stop,* halves the area of the aperture. An increase of one stop from f/5.6 to f/8 (reducing the aperture area by $^1/2$) exactly compensates for doubling the exposure time from, say, $^1/250$ second to $^1/125$ second.

Students may be curious about the rounding that occurs in the shutter speed time scale. If we take the base unit of exposure time to be $^1/1000$ second, sequentially doubling the time (halving the denominator) means that the 1 second mark on the scale actually measures 0.98 seconds. Working from the other direction, repeated halving of an exact 1-second exposure gives us a base unit $^1/1024$ second, which would be recorded on the shutter time scale as 1024. The difference between shutter times of $^1/1024$ and $^1/1000$ is negligible, so 1000 is used as a rounded base unit. Similar rounding produces shutter times of $^1/60$ second, $^1/30$ second, and so on.

Investigation Two • Lenses

Parallel light rays from a distant source (theoretically infinity) are refracted by a lens and converge to meet at a point called the focal point. The distance from the center of the lens to the focal point is called the focal length. By making scale drawings, students investigate the relationship between the focal length of a camera's lens, the distance of an object from the lens, and the distance between the lens and the image of that object on the film. To check the accuracy of their scale drawings, students use the formula

$$\frac{1}{u} + \frac{1}{v} = \frac{1}{f}$$

where u represents the distance between the lens and the object; v, the distance between the lens and the image; and f, the focal length.

Investigation Three • Depth of Field

Depth of field is a measure of just how much of a scene will be in sharp focus for a given level of light and a given f-stop. Students explore the relationship between depth of field, light conditions, and aperture setting: the smaller the f-stop (which requires more light or faster ASA film speed), the greater the depth of field. They also learn that lens quality can affect depth of field; poor quality lenses do not uniformly refract the light due to imperfections in the glass or surface and, therefore, do not have a single focal length for the entire scene. This may narrow the depth of field and make elements in the picture seem out of focus.

Investigation Four • Pattern in the f-Stops

By this point students know that f-stops measure the area of the aperture that lets light through the camera lens. Now they search for a pattern in the sequence of f-stop numbers (1, 1.4, 2, 2.8, and so on), knowing that a single f-stop change either halves or doubles the area of the aperture. The principle involved is this: To double the area of a circular aperture, we multiply the radius by $\sqrt{2}$. [If $A = \pi r^2$, $2A = 2\pi r^2 = \pi(\sqrt{2}r)^2$.] Therefore, since the area of the aperture sequentially decreases by a factor of $1/2$ as f-stops increase, the f-stops are the sequence $\sqrt{2^n}$ for any whole number n. That is, $\sqrt{2^0} = 1$; $\sqrt{2^1} \approx 1.4$; $\sqrt{2^2} = 2$; and so on; or any f-stop times $\sqrt{2}$ equals the next larger f-stop. Students further discover that: *lens focal length ÷ aperture diameter* = f-stop.

Investigation Five • Film Speed

The composition of the film itself is another factor involved in getting a good quality photograph. Different types of film are better in certain light conditions. Film sensitivity, called its *speed,* is measured in ASA (American Standards Association) units; e.g., ASA 50, ASA 100, ASA 400. Doubling the ASA number (say from 100 to 200) means that $1/2$ the light will be required to correctly expose the film. Faster film allows us to use a smaller aperture size for a given light level and therefore gives us greater depth of field and/or allows for a faster shutter speed, useful in getting action photographs that are not blurred. Students investigate the relationship between film speed, light intensity, and the shutter settings for exposure time. They also compare ASA speeds with DIN numbers—the European system that rates film speed in degrees (e.g., DIN 15°).

Investigation Six • Professional Photography

Students explore the proportional relationships among shutter speed, aperture settings, and film speed—some of the variables affecting the quality of a picture. They discover that exposure times and f-stop values are directly proportional, because as the exposure time increases, the f-stop increases (the aperture decreases). Film speed, they discover, is inversely proportional to exposure time and directly proportional to f-stop values. Students are asked to explore *graininess* as it relates to film speed: Faster film is made with larger grains of silver, so the pictures may have less resolution than those taken with slower film.

Investigation One

Shutter Times and f-Stops

1   The film used to take pictures is sensitive to the intensity of light in the scene being photographed. A camera's shutter is like a little window shade that opens and closes very quickly to expose the film to light for a specific period of time. How long the shutter should remain open depends on the intensity of the light reflected from the scene. For less intense light, the shutter must remain open longer to correctly expose the film.

Emily's camera automatically sets the speed of the shutter, or *exposure time,* by measuring the intensity of light in the scene with a built-in light meter. The shutter time-scale is visible in the viewfinder of her camera.

Emily takes a photo of this scene on a sunny afternoon. The time scale in her viewfinder indicates that the film will be exposed for $\frac{1}{250}$ second.

A moment later, Emily takes another picture of the same scene when the sun goes behind a cloud. This shows what she sees in her viewfinder.

a   What exposure time is shown on the scale used for the second photo?

b   Emily reasons that the light intensity halves when the sun goes behind the cloud. Do you think she is correct? Explain your answer.

c Emily notices a pattern in the time scale in her viewfinder and works out this *accurate* table.

  i What pattern did she notice?

  ii Why do you suppose the time scale in the camera is not quite the same as Emily's?

1000
500
250
125
62.5
31.25
15.625
7.8125
3.90625
1.953125
0.9765625

d Suppose we could measure the light intensity in units. Let's say that on a sunny afternoon, when the correct exposure time is $\frac{1}{250}$ second, the light intensity is one unit. Complete the following tables.

i

Exposure Time (s)	Light Intensity (units)
$\frac{1}{250}$	1
$\frac{1}{125}$	$\frac{1}{2}$
$\frac{1}{60}$	
$\frac{1}{30}$	
$\frac{1}{15}$	

ii

Exposure Time (s)	Light Intensity (units)
	$\frac{1}{32}$
	$\frac{1}{64}$
	$\frac{1}{128}$
	2
	4

2 Emily takes two photographs of a street scene in the same light conditions. The exposure times are shown below each picture.

$\frac{1}{500}$ s

$\frac{1}{30}$ s

a Explain why Emily prefers the photo taken at $\frac{1}{500}$ s.

b Photographers are advised not to use an exposure time longer than $\frac{1}{30}$ s without the use of a *tripod,* a three-legged support that holds a camera steady. Explain the reasoning behind this advice.

← Tripod

3 Another way a photographer can control the amount of light that exposes the film is by changing the *aperture* setting. The aperture is an adjustable hole in a diaphragm covering the lens. Making the hole smaller blocks some of the light passing through the lens. Thus a large aperture lets more light into the camera than a small aperture.

The size of the aperture is measured in units called f-stops: f/1.4, f/2, f/2.8, f/4, f/5.6, f/8, f/11, f/16. The larger the number, the smaller the size of the aperture. On some cameras, you will see these numbers on one of the rings around the lens. By turning this ring, you can set the aperture to any f-stop.

Apertures

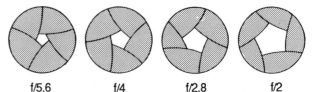

f/5.6 f/4 f/2.8 f/2

Because both the shutter speed and the aperture are used to control the light that exposes the film, changing one setting will affect the other setting.

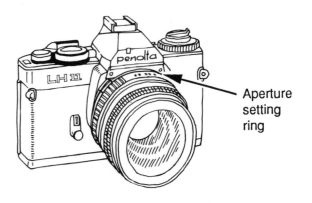

Aperture setting ring

While preparing to take a photograph, Emily uses the lens ring to set the aperture to f/4. She notices that the exposure time shown automatically in her viewfinder is $\frac{1}{15}$ s. Emily remembers the advice that this time is too long for her to hold the camera steady without a tripod, so she changes the f-stop by one stop from f/4 to f/2.8.

When she sees that the automatic exposure time is now $\frac{1}{30}$ s, Emily concludes that the area of the f/2.8 aperture is *double* the area of the f/4 aperture.

The manual for a camera states:

> **A decrease in the f-number by one stop doubles the size, or area, of the aperture. So, for a correct exposure, the exposure time must be halved.**

a Explain why this is true.

b Complete the following tables to show how exposure times change as Emily changes the f-stop, or aperture size.

i

f-stop	Exposure Time (s)
4	$\frac{1}{15}$
2.8	
2	
1.4	

ii

f-stop	Exposure Time (s)
	$\frac{1}{8}$
	$\frac{1}{4}$
	$\frac{1}{2}$
	1

c The relation between the f-stop and the exposure time will depend on the light intensity at any given time. In different light conditions, Emily notices that with a setting of f/5.6, the exposure time is $\frac{1}{125}$ s.

Complete the following tables to show how the exposure time will change as she changes the aperture size.

i

f-stop	Exposure Time (s)
5.6	$\frac{1}{125}$
8	
11	
16	

ii

f-stop	ExposureTime (s)
4	
2.8	
2	
1.4	

4 a Complete the next table, assuming that light conditions remain constant.

b In this light, which combination of f-stop and exposure time would you use for photographing a car race? Explain your answer.

f-stop	ExposureTime (s)
8	$\frac{1}{125}$
11	
16	
5.6	
4	
2.8	

c   Complete the following six tables, which show the relation between
    f- stops and exposure times in a variety of light conditions.

i   Midday—sunny

f-stop	Exposure Time (s)
16	$\frac{1}{30}$
11	
8	
5.6	
4	

ii Midday—cloudy

f-stop	Exposure Time (s)
16	$\frac{1}{15}$
11	
8	
5.6	
4	

iii Dawn

f-stop	Exposure Time (s)
16	
11	
8	
5.6	
4	$\frac{1}{60}$

iv Misty

f-stop	Exposure Time (s)
8	$\frac{1}{8}$
2	

v   Raining

f-stop	Exposure Time (s)
8	$\frac{1}{30}$
	$\frac{1}{8}$

vi Sunset

f-stop	Exposure Time (s)
16	$\frac{1}{4}$
	$\frac{1}{60}$

5   Meredith wants to take a photo of a champion racehorse in action
    in poor light conditions. She sets the aperture to f/2.8 and notes
    the exposure time of $\frac{1}{30}$ s in the viewfinder. She wants to use $\frac{1}{250}$ s
    to avoid a blurred photograph.

   a   i   What f-stop does she need?
       ii Is this f-stop possible?

   b   Can Meredith find a way to take
          the photograph?

Investigation Two

Lenses

1 Vanessa uses a magnifying glass to ignite a piece of paper to start a campfire. She adjusts the distance of the lens from the paper until the sun's rays come together in sharp focus to form the smallest possible dot on the paper. This point is called the *focal point,* and the distance between this point and the center of the lens is called the *focal length* of the lens. Different lenses have different focal lengths.

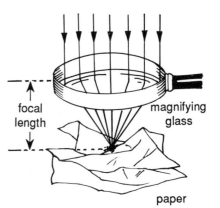

Use Vanessa's method to find the focal length of a magnifying glass. For safety, use the light from a lamp instead of the sun to avoid risking a burn.

2 A camera's lens is like a magnifying glass. If you hold a magnifying glass at arm's length, the image you see through the lens is upside down. Similarly, light rays reflected from a object you plan to photograph are bent by the camera's lens and are "projected" upside down on the film behind the lens.

The following diagram of a camera helps explain why the image of the object (represented by arrow AB) is inverted on the film.

O = center of lens
F = focal point
f = focal length
AB = object being photographed
B'A' = inverted image of object on film

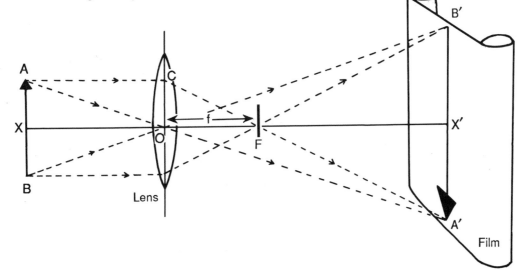

Suppose a camera lens has a focal length of 40 mm (as shown in the diagram below).

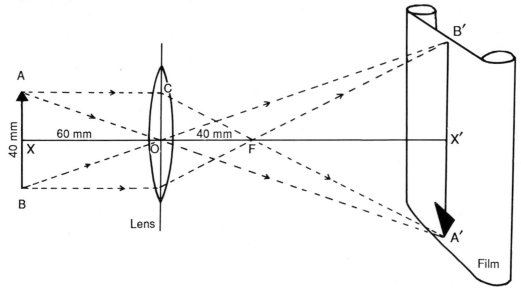

a Why does light ray AC bend to pass through the focal point F? (If you can't explain this, look in a photography reference book.)

b AOA′ is nearly a straight line. Explain why. (Again, a reference book may help.)

c Use graph paper and a millimeter ruler to make an accurate drawing of the above example, showing exactly the position and length of B′A′—the inverted image of arrow AB.

d For the following examples **i-iv**, use graph paper to make accurate drawings and measure the distance from the image B′A′ to the center of the lens (the length of X′O).

i Focal length = 30 mm

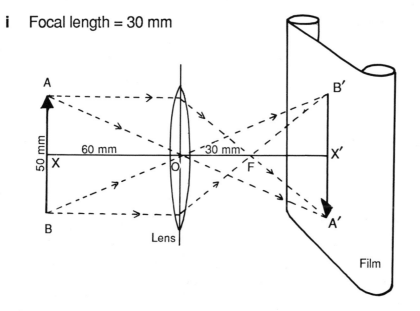

ii Focal length = 40 mm

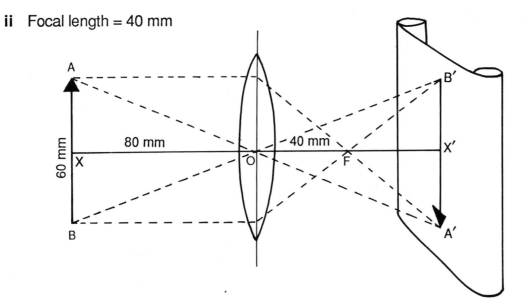

iii Focal length = 30 mm

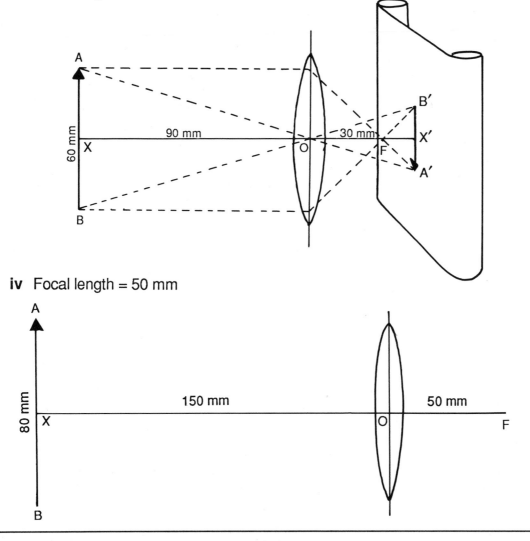

iv Focal length = 50 mm

e Test your results in **d** to see if they fit the lens formula

$$\frac{1}{u} + \frac{1}{v} = \frac{1}{f}$$

where u = length of XO,
v = length of X'O,
and f = focal length.

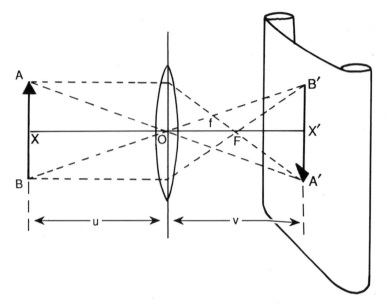

f Explain why the image of an object a very large distance from a camera is located at a distance behind the lens equal to the focal length of the lens. (*Hint:* Use the formula given in **e**.)

3 Some cameras have an automatic focus, but others are focused by turning a ring around the lens. When the focusing ring is turned, the lens in the camera moves backwards or forwards. Notice that the distance v in the lens formula changes as the focusing ring is turned.

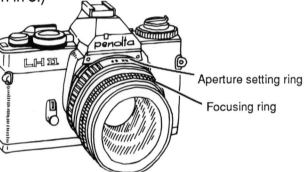

Aperture setting ring

Focusing ring

a Why is a focusing ring necessary?

b Suppose an object (AB) is 360 mm from the film at the back of the camera. The focal length of the lens is 50 mm.

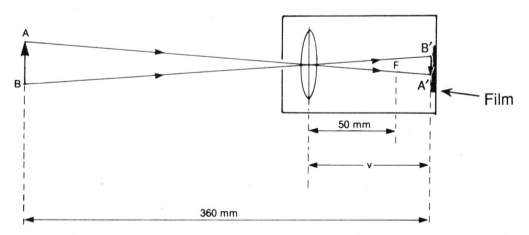

Use the lens formula to find the distance, v, of the lens from the film.

Investigation Three

Depth of Field

1 Photographers use the phrase *depth of field* to tell how much of a given scene, from the camera to the horizon, is going to be in focus when a picture is taken.

When a person standing close to the camera is in focus and everything behind the person is out of focus, we say that the picture has a *narrow* depth of field. In a picture with a *broad* depth of field, *all* objects are in focus, from those near the camera to those on the horizon.

Michael took two photographs while standing in one spot, using the same focus setting but different apertures (f-stops) and corresponding shutter times. He took one picture at f/4 and the other at f/16. In the diagrams below (representing these pictures), only the dark figures are in focus.

a Which of the two pictures has a greater depth of field?

b The diagrams below show a side view of the scene in Michael's photographs. For each f-stop he used, indicate the extent of the region that is in focus.

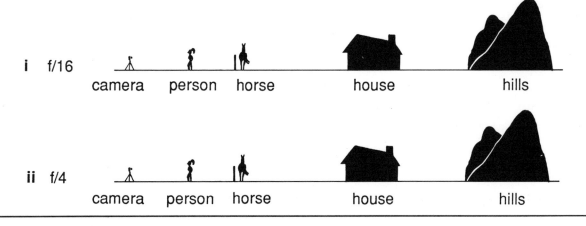

i f/16   camera   person   horse   house   hills

ii f/4   camera   person   horse   house   hills

O*N YOUR OWN*

Obtain a camera with a lens that can be focused.

1 Find the markings on the lens that show the depth of field and work out how to use them.

2 If the camera you found is a Single-Lens Reflex (SLR) type, investigate whether the camera has some mechanism for previewing the depth of field of a photo before you take it.

3 Explain why rangefinder or Twin-Lens Reflex cameras do not permit a preview of the depth of field before a photo is taken.

2 Michael is curious about why the depth of field changes as the aperture changes. He draws a diagram for a camera lens with a focal length of 40 mm, showing the image of the tree AB focused on the film. (Diagram 1.)

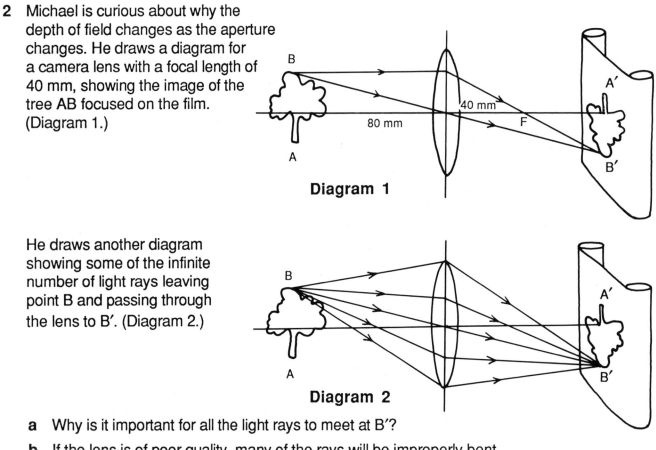

Diagram 1

He draws another diagram showing some of the infinite number of light rays leaving point B and passing through the lens to B′. (Diagram 2.)

Diagram 2

a Why is it important for all the light rays to meet at B′?

b If the lens is of poor quality, many of the rays will be improperly bent and will strike the film too far from B′. What would a photo taken with such a poor lens look like?

c Draw a sketch like Diagram 2, showing the rays starting at point A and finishing at A′.

d Suggest a way of defining the quality of a photographic lens.

e Slightly beyond AB is another tree DG. D is a point on this tree's trunk. Michael finds D′ by carefully drawing rays 1 and 2 in Diagram 3 (as you did in the last investigation).

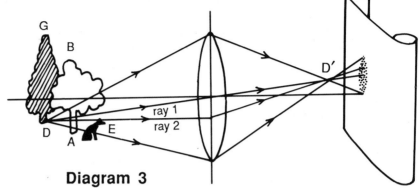

Diagram 3

Explain why the image of point D will not appear as a tiny dot on the film, but as a solid circle.

f How do you think tree DG will look on the film?

g Michael then draws Diagram 4, which shows what happens when a smaller aperture reduces the lens to a narrow 20 mm diameter.

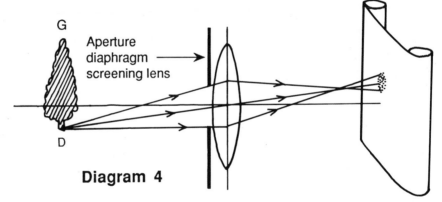

Diagram 4

Compare the images of point D shown in Diagrams 3 and 4. In which case will the image appear more blurred (less focused)?

h In Diagram 3, a dog is sitting slightly in front of tree AB. Point E is the tip of the dog's nose. Draw a sketch showing how point E will appear on the film.

i Draw a sketch like Diagram 4, showing what point E will look like when a smaller aperture reduces the lens to a 20 mm diameter.

j Compare your answers in **h** and **i**.

3 For a normal human eye, the closest comfortable focusing distance from an object is about 250 mm (or about 10 inches). At this distance, a circle with a 0.2 mm diameter appears to be a single point. Use these facts and your answers to problem **2** to explain why the depth of field increases as the aperture of a camera is reduced.

Investigation Four

Patterns in the f-Stops

1 Zachary sees a table of f-stops in a photographer's manual. (Note that most cameras do not have an f-stop of 1.)

   a The accurate f-stops have been *truncated* to give approximate f-stops. Is this a sensible thing to do?

   b **i** Find a pattern in the accurate f-stops.
      ii What might explain why f-stops have this pattern?

f-stops	
Approximate	**Accurate**
1	1
1.4	1.414 213 6
2	2
2.8	2.828 427 1
4	4
5.6	5.656 854 25
8	8
11	11.313 708
16	16
22	22.627 417

2 A 50-mm lens is set at f/4. At this setting, the aperture area—which is close enough to a circle to be considered such—is 123 mm² (to three significant figures).

   a **i** Elena claims the area of the aperture for f/2.8 is 246 mm². Explain her reasoning.
      ii Complete the following table for a lens with a focal length of 50 mm.

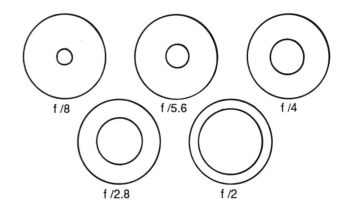

f/8   f/5.6   f/4

f/2.8   f/2

f-stop	Area of Aperture (mm²) (unrounded)	Diameter of Aperture (mm) (unrounded)	Focal Length of Lens ÷ Diameter of Aperture (two significant figures)
1.4			
2			
2.8	246		
4	123		
5.6			
8			
11			
16			

b For a lens with an 85-mm focal length, the area of the aperture at f/4 is 355 mm² (to three significant figures). Make a table for this lens similar to the one in **a ii** and complete it.

c Write a formula that links the f-stop, the aperture's diameter, and the focal length of a lens.

d Complete the following tables. (Round sensibly.)

   f = focal length

   d = aperture diameter

i

f (mm)	d (mm)	f-stop
100	50	
100	71	
100	9	
56	10	
400	100	

ii

f (mm)	d (mm)	f-stop
	35	2
	12	5.6
	5	16
90		11
200		4
400		2.8

CLASS INVESTIGATION

Suppose two lenses with focal lengths of 200 mm and 50 mm are focused on a distant object.

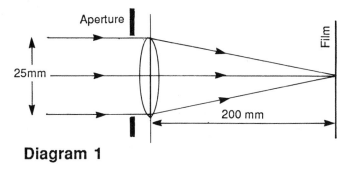

Diagram 1

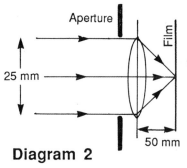

Diagram 2

1 Explain why *less* intense light falls on the film in Diagram 1.

2 Explain why the aperture in Diagram 1 should be 100 mm for the same intensity of light as in Diagram 2. Calculate the f-stops for both lenses in this case. What do you notice?

3 A photographer sets the aperture for a 55-mm lens at f/5.6. She decides to change the lens for a 200-mm telephoto lens. What f-stops should she use? (Check by experiment if you can.)

*O*NYOUROWN

List the f-stops for a variety of camera lenses. Find any variations from the f-stops ... 1.4, 2, 2.8, ..., 16, ... and comment on your results.

3 a Suppose A11 is the aperture area at f/11, A8 the area at f/8, and so on. Explain why the following flowchart is correct for *any* camera lens.

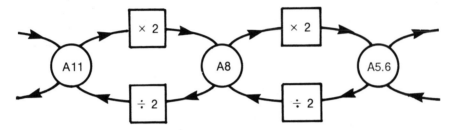

   b In this diagram, the area of the small square is doubled.
   i Find the length of the side of each square.

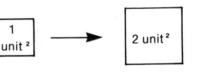

   ii In the flowchart below, d11 is the aperture diameter at f/11, d8 is the diameter at f/8, and so on. Use your answers to **a** and **b i** to explain why the following flowchart is correct for any camera lens.

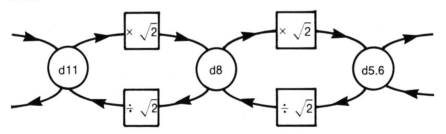

   c In the flowchart below, the f-stops are shown in the circles.
   i Check that the flowchart is correct.

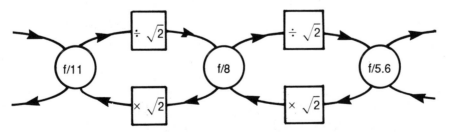

   ii Compare the flowcharts in **b ii** and **c i**. What do you notice? Can you explain any differences?

Investigation Five

Film Speed

1 A photographer can buy film of different *speeds,* rated in ASA (American Standards Association) units. A film with a high ASA rating is more sensitive to light than one with a lower ASA. A camera must be set to reflect the ASA rating of the film being used because the film speed will affect the other settings.

Suppose that on a bright day, 100 ASA film is correctly exposed at f/4 and $\frac{1}{60}$ s by 1 unit of light. A faster film rated 200 ASA has twice the light sensitivity (speed) of 100 ASA film and is correctly exposed by $\frac{1}{2}$ unit of light.

Film speed (ASA) x	Light Required for Correct Exposure (units) y
25	
50	
100	1
200	$\frac{1}{2}$
400	
800	
1600	

a Complete the table.

b Use the pattern in the table to complete the following rule:

$$y = \frac{\Box}{x}$$

c Use the rule from **b** to determine the values for *y* as shown in this table. (Round to two significant figures.)

x	y
80	
150	
600	
1000	

On Your Own

1 Find out when photographers use the following:

    a Slow film (20–40 ASA)

    b Medium speed film (80–200 ASA)

    c Fast film (400+ ASA)

2 What is the major disadvantage of fast film?

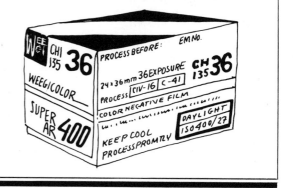

2 Instead of ASA, some countries use the German standard DIN rating system for film speed.

a Use patterns to complete the table of film speed equivalents.

b Graph the data in the table.

c Use your graph to *estimate* the DIN rating for the following films.
   i   40 ASA
   ii 64 ASA
   iii 500 ASA

Film Speed Equivalents	
ASA	DIN
25	
50	
100	21°
200	24°
400	27°
	30°
	33°

d Let x = film speed in ASA and y = film speed in DIN. Substitute values from the table and show that the following formulas fit the data. Remember, first calculate the amount in parentheses (in this case the exponent), then work out the power of two, and finally multiply the results.

   i $x = 100 \times 2^{(y-21)/3}$
   ii $x = 50 \times 2^{(y-18)/3}$
   iii $x = 200 \times 2^{(y-24)/3}$

e Make up more formulas like the ones in d.

f Does film have both the ASA and DIN ratings printed on the box it is packed in? (Check several different brands, if possible.)

g If $\frac{1}{2}$ unit of light is needed to correctly expose 24° film, how many units of light will be needed to correctly expose 30° film?

3 Jody puts 100 ASA film in her camera and sets the automatic light meter for this film speed. In bright sunlight, her meter indicates that she needs an exposure time of $\frac{1}{250}$ s. The light intensity drops as the sun goes down.

a i   Explain why Jody will use an exposure time of $\frac{1}{125}$ s when the light intensity is half of the initial reading.

   ii Complete the table. (Assume that Jody keeps the f-stop the same.)

Fraction of Bright Light	Exposure Time (s)
1	$\frac{1}{250}$
$\frac{1}{2}$	$\frac{1}{125}$
$\frac{1}{4}$	
$\frac{1}{8}$	
	$\frac{1}{15}$
$\frac{1}{32}$	$\frac{1}{8}$
	$\frac{1}{4}$

b What speed film could Jody have used to maintain an exposure time of $\frac{1}{250}$ s when the light intensity is half the initial reading?

c Complete the following tables, which show the relation between film speed and exposure time in a variety of light conditions. Assume that the f-stops do not change.

i Midday—sunny

ASA	Exposure Time (s)
200	$\frac{1}{500}$
100	$\frac{1}{250}$
50	
25	

ii Overcast

ASA	Exposure Time (s)
200	$\frac{1}{125}$
100	
50	
25	

iii Dusk

ASA	Exposure Time (s)
200	
100	$\frac{1}{15}$
50	
25	

iv Raining

ASA	Exposure Time (s)
100	$\frac{1}{60}$
	$\frac{1}{125}$
	$\frac{1}{250}$
	$\frac{1}{500}$

v Dawn

ASA	Exposure Time (s)
	$\frac{1}{4}$
	$\frac{1}{8}$
1600	$\frac{1}{15}$
	$\frac{1}{30}$

vi Dull afternoon

ASA	Exposure Time (s)
	$\frac{1}{15}$
	$\frac{1}{30}$
200	$\frac{1}{60}$
	$\frac{1}{125}$

4 Yoshio has a simple camera with a fixed shutter (exposure) time. He can vary both the aperture and the film speed. He has bought a roll of 100 ASA film. The film instruction sheet advises him to use f/8 to take a picture in the shade on a sunny day. When the weather is heavily overcast, he estimates that the light intensity is one-fourth of the light intensity in the shade on a sunny day.

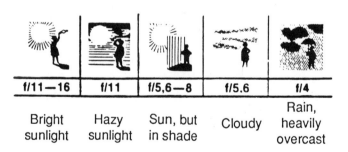

f/11—16	f/11	f/5,6—8	f/5.6	f/4
Bright sunlight	Hazy sunlight	Sun, but in shade	Cloudy	Rain, heavily overcast

a i What ASA film should Yoshio use to get the correct exposure on a heavily overcast day with an aperture setting of f/8?

ii Is the solution in **a i** practical?

b Yoshio decides not to change the 100 ASA film in his camera.

    i On a heavily overcast day, he sets the aperture at f/4. Why does he use this setting?

    ii What effect will such a change in aperture setting have on the depth of field?

    iii Do you think Yoshio made a wise decision not to change the film in his camera before taking the photograph?

c Using 50 ASA film, Yoshio finds that a setting of f/4 gives a correct exposure for light intensity of $\frac{1}{4}$ unit. Complete the table for Yoshio's camera.

25 ASA		50 ASA		100 ASA		200 ASA	
Light Intensity	f-stop	Light Intensity	f-stop	Light Intensity	f-stop	Light Intensity	f-stop
$\frac{1}{4}$		$\frac{1}{4}$	4	$\frac{1}{4}$	5.6	$\frac{1}{4}$	
$\frac{1}{2}$		$\frac{1}{2}$		$\frac{1}{2}$		$\frac{1}{2}$	
1		1		1		1	

5 **a** In certain light conditions, if you are using 200 ASA film, a setting of f/8 will give the correct exposure. Complete the tables for these conditions.

i

ASA	f-stop
200	8
100	
50	
25	

ii

ASA	f-stop
200	8
400	
800	
1600	

b Suppose that, in certain light conditions, you are using 100 ASA film and the setting f/11 results in the correct exposure for a photograph. What would be the correct f-stop if you were using 25 ASA film in the same light conditions?

Investigation Six

Professional Photography

1 With 100 ASA film in her camera, Shelley takes two photos from the same place, using different f-stops and exposure times.

Photo A
f/11, $\frac{1}{30}$ second

Photo B
f/4, $\frac{1}{250}$ second

a Why do you suppose photo A has a greater depth of field than photo B?

b As photographer for her local paper, Shelley has been assigned to take photos at the beach volleyball championships. She uses a small aperture setting to give her pictures a large depth of field. Why is this necessary for most sports photography?

c She also sets a fast shutter speed for a short exposure time. Why is this common in photographing sports action?

d Suppose the weather at the beach volleyball championships is overcast. Why would Shelley choose 800 ASA (very fast) film?

e Ramon wonders why Shelley does not use fast film for all her work. Shelley says she likes to use slow film for studio portraits because it is less grainy. Describe what you think a *grainy* photo might look like. Talk to a photographer or check in a photography book to see if you are right.

2 Danny's light meter indicates that, with 200 ASA film, he should set his camera at f/2.8 and $\frac{1}{60}$ s.

a Danny reasons that settings of f/4 at $\frac{1}{30}$ s will also be correct. Explain his reasoning.

b Complete the table.

c Which combination of settings would be best for an action sports photo?

d Which combination of settings would be best for landscapes?

e Why would a photographer use a tripod with an f/8 setting in these conditions?

f-stop	Exposure Time (s)
1.4	
2	
2.8	$\frac{1}{60}$
4	$\frac{1}{30}$
5.6	
8	
11	

3 a Suppose a photo will be correctly exposed using 400 ASA film with an aperture setting of f/8 and an exposure time of $\frac{1}{60}$ s. Complete the following tables for correct exposures. Assume the lighting conditions are constant throughout.

i

ASA	f-stop	Exposure Time (s)
400	8	$\frac{1}{60}$
200	8	
100	8	
50	8	
50		$\frac{1}{15}$
50		$\frac{1}{8}$
50		$\frac{1}{4}$
50		$\frac{1}{2}$

ii

ASA	f-stop	Exposure Time (s)
400	8	$\frac{1}{60}$
200		$\frac{1}{60}$
100		$\frac{1}{60}$
50		$\frac{1}{60}$
100	2.8	
200	2.8	
400	2.8	
800	2.8	

b A photographer has four films of different speeds available. He can set his camera for 9 different f-stops and 11 exposure times. How many different combinations of film speed, aperture setting, and exposure time can he use?

CHECK-UP

1 A certain wide-angle lens (sometimes called a "fish-eye" lens) has a focal length of 17 mm.

    a What is the aperture diameter at f/4?

    b **i** Comment on the depth of field for this lens at f/4.

       ii Use your answer to **b i** to explain how you might use this lens.

2 **a** Suppose 1 unit of light is needed to correctly expose DIN 21° film (100 ASA). How many units of light will be needed to correctly expose the following?

       i DIN 27° film

       ii 50 ASA film

    b Nick uses DIN 33° film. Find the ASA equivalent, using the formula

$$x = 100 \times 2^{(y-21)/3}$$

    where x = ASA and y = DIN film speed.

3 Sonja is going to take a picture with 400 ASA film. Her light meter indicates that for the correct exposure, she should set her camera at f/5.6 and $\frac{1}{125}$ s.

    a In order to increase the depth of field, she changes the aperture setting to f/11. What shutter speed should she now set for correct exposure?

    b **i** What shutter speed should be set for correct exposure at f/16?

       ii Sonja would have increased the depth of field even further with an f/16 aperture setting. Why didn't she use this setting?

    c Suppose Sonja is going to photograph some sports action. In buying film, which speed should she select? Explain your answer.

CHAPTER FIVE

GENETICS

TEACHING NOTES

The study of the inheritance of genetic traits in humans employs systematic counting and probability. In this chapter, students explore the mathematics underlying the transmittal of certain human characteristics and diseases from one generation to the next.

Investigation One • Inheritance

The basic principle in this section is that a dominant gene overpowers an associated recessive gene. For example, the "round-face" gene G_F is dominant over the "thin-face" gene G_f. If two round-faced parents each contribute a dominant and recessive face-shape gene (and there is an equal chance for each gene to be contributed), there is a $3/4$ probability that each of their offspring will have a round face. The possible gene pairings (all equally likely) are *round/round, round/thin,* and *thin/round,* all giving a round-faced offspring, and *thin/thin,* giving a thin-faced offspring. Students are introduced to *inheritance diagrams* for the systematic listing of gene pairs and use these diagrams along with deductive reasoning to make decisions about the probability that offspring will inherit specific traits. They investigate inheritance patterns for the genes responsible for such traits as round/thin face; wide/narrow eyes; Rh+/Rh− blood factors; freckles/no freckles; thin flat nails/normal nails; thick lips/thin lips; early-graying hair/normal hair.

Investigation Two • Blood Types

Blood classifications are type A, type B, and type AB (all dominant) and type O (recessive). Students use a table to organize possible blood types and use the results to work inheritance problems and to analyze population immigration patterns.

Investigation Three • Inherited Diseases

Students explore Huntington's chorea (dominant gene), phenylketonuria or PKU (recessive gene), and other inherited diseases, using inheritance tables to determine the likelihood of parents' passing such diseases on to their offspring. Similarly, students use inheritance tables to calculate from family histories the probability that a given individual has the disease.

Investigation Four • Gender-Linked Diseases

Students investigate the special role of the gender-determining chromosome pair (XX = female; XY = male) in this section. They find that hemophilia, a disorder that leads to uncontrollable bleeding, is caused by a recessive non-clotting gene. Genes related to blood clotting are attached only to the X chromosome, never the Y. Since females have two X chromosomes, they are likely to have a dominant blood-clotting gene that will overpower a recessive non-clotting gene. However, males who have a recessive non-clotting gene attached to their X chromosome have no chance of attaining a second clotting gene since their gender-determining chromosome pair is XY (that is, they do not have a second X chromosome). Students use their knowledge of gene inheritance to explain why this disease is found almost exclusively in males. They also investigate inheritance patterns for color-blindness, another recessive trait that disproportionally affects males since the Y chromosome carries no genes related to vision.

Investigation One

Inheritance

Most human cells have 23 pairs of chromosomes (46 total). One chromosome in each pair is inherited from the father, the other from the mother. Each chromosome has many genes, which we can think of as manufacturing sites where individual human characteristics such as eye color, stature, and skin color are determined. Seen under a high-powered microscope, chromosomes look like the thread-like bodies shown here. For simplicity, we will picture them in these investigations as rectangular rods.

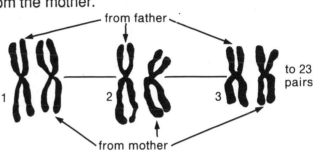

1 John inherits the genes for a round face from *both* his parents, so he has a round face. He marries Anne, who has inherited the genes for a thin face from *both* her parents.

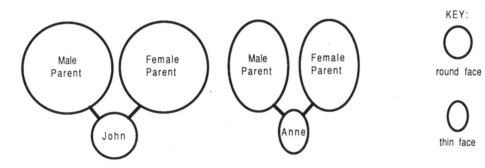

KEY:

○ round face

○ thin face

A biology student draws chromosome models for John and Anne.

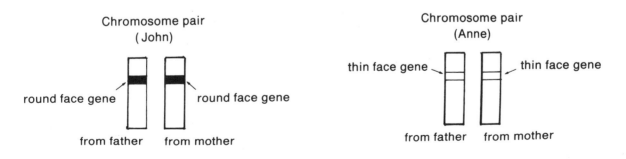

Each of John and Anne's children has a round face, so the biology student concludes that the gene for a round face is *dominant* over the gene for a thin face, which must be *recessive*.

The biology student draws the following diagram to explain the inheritance of these dominant/recessive genes. (*D* stands for dominant and *r* for recessive. Germ cells are contributed by each parent when a child is conceived.)

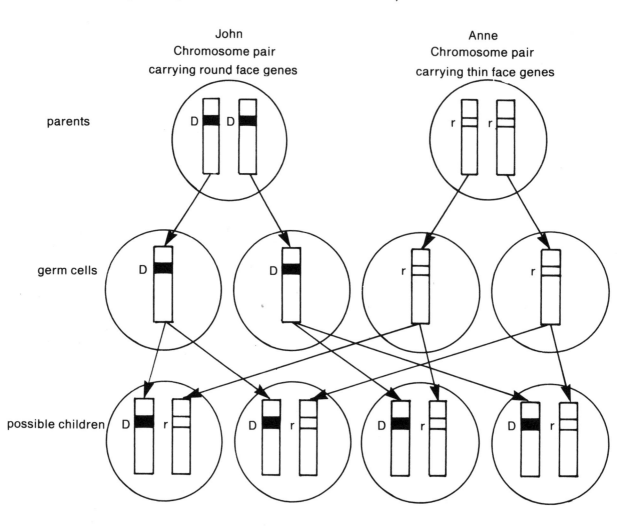

a See if you can explain how the diagram works.

b One of their children, Rachel, marries Jack, who is round faced but carries the thin-face gene recessively. Starting out as shown at the right, draw a diagram showing the thin-face/round-face genes for Rachel and Jack's possible children.

c Explain why the probability that Rachel and Jack will have a thin-faced baby is $\frac{1}{4}$.

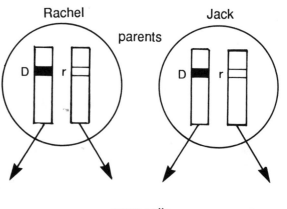

2 In practice, it is difficult to know whether a person carries recessive genes. However, some clues can be found by looking at that person's children.

a Doug and Ashley both have wide eyes. However, their first child has narrow eyes, which is a recessive trait. Complete the chart below. Start with their firstborn and work backward, then forward again. Be sure to mark each chromosome either dominant (D) or recessive (r).

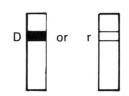

 Wide eyes dominant

 Narrow eyes recessive

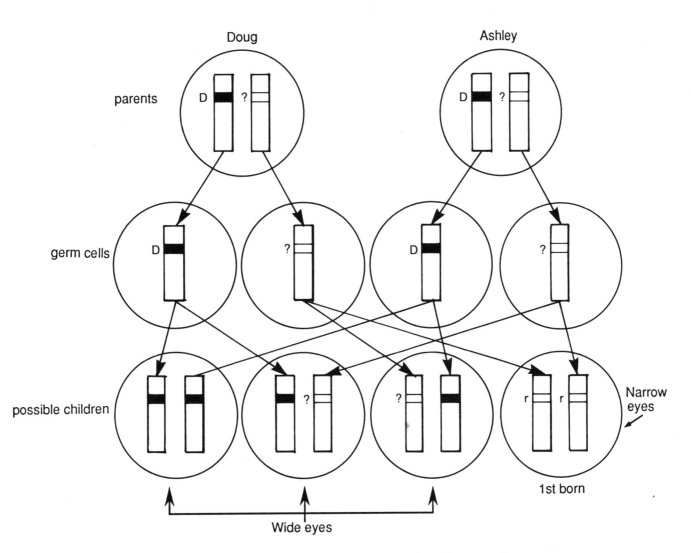

b Assuming the same situation, what is the probability that Doug and Ashley's second child has:
  i narrow eyes?
  ii wide eyes and is carrying the recessive gene for narrow eyes?
  iii wide eyes and is not carrying the recessive gene for narrow eyes?

3 An important aspect of everyone's blood is its *Rh factor* (or *Rhesus factor,* named after the kind of monkey in which this factor was first discovered). All people are either Rh positive (having the Rh factor) or Rh negative (lacking the Rh factor).

> **Rh Factor of Blood**
> gene for positive (Rh+) — dominant
> gene for negative (Rh−) — recessive

a Occasionally, a pregnant woman's blood will react with her unborn baby's blood with disastrous results for her baby. Find out how the Rh factor is involved in this phenomenon and how it can be prevented.

b Heidi is Rh+ (Rh factor positive), and so is her husband Todd. Their firstborn, Charlotte, is Rh−. Draw an inheritance diagram to explain how this can happen.

c Charlotte marries Jake, who is Rh+. Their firstborn is Rh−. Is Jake carrying the Rh− gene recessively? Explain your answer with an inheritance diagram.

d Deirdre and Sean, who are both Rh−, have a child named Marie who claims she must be adopted because she is Rh+. Can Sean be her father? Explain your answer.

4 Instead of drawing gene diagrams, Erika devises a gene inheritance table. She uses it to investigate inheritance of the gene for freckles.

Marci has freckles and so does her mother, Heidi. Marci's father Todd has no freckles.

> G_F = gene for freckles — dominant
> G_f = gene for no freckles — recessive

a Explain why Todd must be G_fG_f.

b Explain why Heidi must be G_FG_f or G_FG_F.

c As Erika made her table (shown at right), she assumed that Heidi is G_FG_f. Using the table, she predicted that the probability that any child of Todd and Heidi will have freckles is $\frac{1}{2}$. Explain how she determined this.

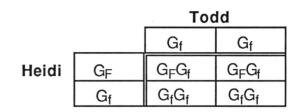

		Todd	
		G_f	G_f
Heidi	G_F	G_FG_f	G_FG_f
	G_f	G_fG_f	G_fG_f

d **i** Make a table like Erika's, but assume that Heidi is G_FG_F.

   ii In this case, what is the probability that a child of Heidi and Todd will have freckles?

e In fact, Heidi and Todd have another daughter, Charlotte, who does *not* have freckles. Which of the tables *must* be correct?

5 Let G_T = gene for thin flat nails and G_t = gene for normal fingernails. Hazel has normal nails. Her mother has thin flat nails. Her father has normal nails.

G_T = gene for thin flat nails — dominant
G_t = gene for normal nails — recessive

a Complete the gene inheritance table for Hazel's family.

b What is the probability that her parents' *next* child will have normal nails?

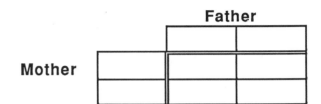

c Norman has thin flat nails. His father has thin flat nails. His mother has normal nails. He also has a sister with normal nails.

i Prepare a gene inheritance table for Norman's family.

ii What is the probability that Norman's next-born sibling (brother or sister) will have normal nails?

6 Howard has thick lips. His father has thin lips, and his mother has thick lips. Howard has five brothers and sisters, all of whom have thick lips.

G_L = gene for thick lips — dominant
G_l = gene for thin lips — recessive

a Howard is certain that his father is G_lG_l and that his mother is almost certainly G_LG_L rather than G_LG_l. Explain his reasoning.

b Assuming that Howard's reasoning is correct, Howard himself must be G_LG_l. Explain why.

c Howard marries Maureen, who has thin lips. They plan to have six children. How many of their children, on average, would you expect to have thin lips?

7 Jim's hair had turned gray by the time he was 25. Stephanie still has black hair at age 40. They have two children. Assume Jim is G_GG_g.

G_G = gene for gray hair by age 25 — dominant
G_g = gene for gray hair in old age — recessive

a What is the probability that their firstborn will have gray hair by age 25?

b What is the probability that *both* their children will have gray hair by age 25?

ON YOUR OWN

The dominant-recessive model used in this inheritance investigation is usually correct. More complex biological theories are needed to explain why the simple dominant-recessive model sometimes breaks down. Read about these more complex theories and write a brief summary.

ON YOUR OWN

Use this table to explore human inheritance. Think of how you might apply the information to people you know.

Human characteristics often inherited

DOMINANT	RECESSIVE	DOMINANT	RECESSIVE
BROAD SKULL	NARROW SKULL	STRAIGHT NOSE	CONCAVE NOSE
ROUND FACE	LONG FACE	NARROW NOSE	WIDE NOSE
STRAIGHT EYES	OBLIQUE EYES	BROWN HAIR	BLONDE HAIR
TONGUE ROLLER	NON-TONGUE ROLLER	RED HAIR	BLONDE HAIR
WIDE EYES	NARROW EYES	FRIZZLED HAIR	CURLY, WAVY OR STRAIGHT HAIR
LONG EYELASHES	SHORT EYELASHES	CURLY HAIR	WAVY OR STRAIGHT HAIR
DROOPING EYELIDS	NORMAL EYELIDS	WAVY HAIR	STRAIGHT HAIR
LONG NOSE	MEDIUM OR SMALL NOSE	ERECT HAIR	LANK HAIR
POINTED NOSE	NORMAL NOSE	WIDE NOSTRILS	NARROW NOSTRILS
HOOKED NOSE	STRAIGHT NOSE	GRAY HAIR AT AGE 25	GRAY HAIR IN OLD AGE

Investigation Two

Blood Types

1 The main blood classifications are type A, type B, and type O. Since G_A and G_B are both dominant, $G_A G_B$ produces an additional blood type, type AB.

G_A = gene for blood type A — dominant

G_B = gene for blood type B — dominant

G_O = gene for blood type O — recessive

a Complete the following gene-pairing table. The resultant blood type for each gene pairing is given in the bottom right section of each table cell.

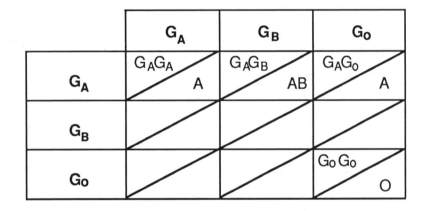

b Ross has blood type A and Jocelyn has blood type B.
  i Explain why a chromosome pair for Ross's blood genes must be one of the two shown here.
  ii What are the possible gene pairings for Jocelyn?

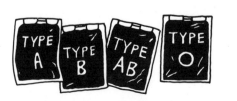

On YOUR OWN

Find out what types of blood can be used in blood transfusions for patients of each of the four different blood types.

iii Suppose Ross is $G_A G_A$ and Jocelyn is $G_B G_O$. Complete the gene diagram below to determine the possible blood types their children will have.

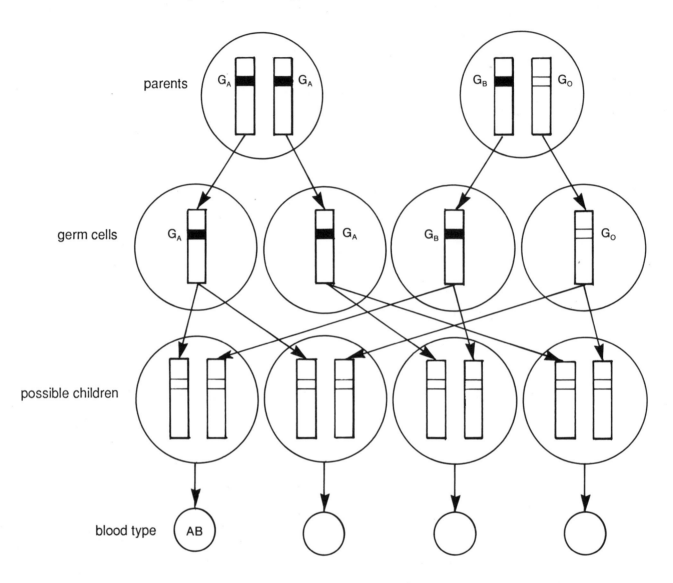

iv Complete this gene inheritance table for Ross and Jocelyn.

		Ross			
		$G_A G_A$		$G_A G_O$	
		G_A	G_A	G_A	G_O
$G_B G_B$	G_B				
	G_B				
$G_B G_O$	G_B	$G_B G_A$	$G_B G_A$		
	G_O	$G_O G_A$	$G_O G_A$		

Jocelyn

v Ross and Jocelyn have a child with blood type O. Use your completed table to prove that Ross is $G_A G_O$ and Jocelyn is $G_B G_O$.

c Denise has blood type AB and Richard has blood type B.
  i Explain why Denise is $G_A G_B$ and Richard is either $G_B G_B$ or $G_B G_O$.

Richard

		$G_B G_B$		$G_B G_O$	
		G_B	G_B	G_B	G_O
Denise $G_A G_B$	G_A	$G_A G_B$	$G_A G_B$		
	G_B	$G_B G_B$	$G_B G_B$		

  ii One of Denise and Richard's children has blood type A. Prove that Richard is $G_B G_O$. (Complete the table if this helps you.)

d Vicki has blood type O and her husband Bill has blood type AB. The hospital mixes up two newborn children. One child has blood type O. Prove that this child cannot belong to Vicki and Bill.

e Dawn has blood type A and Steve has blood type B. Their son claims he must be adopted since he has blood type O. Examine his claim. Does it have any merit?

2 a For each case shown in the table, deduce as much as you can about the gene pairings of each parent.

Blood Type			Genes	
Father	Mother	Child	Father	Mother
O	A	O	$G_O G_O$	$G_A G_O$
A	B	O		
O	O	O		
O	B	B		

b The blood types of three more family groups are described below. For each family, deduce what the parents' gene-pairings must be.
  i Father has type A blood. Mother has type AB blood. Their son has type B blood.
  ii Father has type A blood. Mother has type B blood. Their daughter has type AB blood and their son type O.
  iii Father has type O blood. Mother has type B blood. All their six children have type B blood.

3

| | Australian Aborigines | | | | | Papua New Guinea | Indo-nesia |
	Cape York	S.E. Queensland	Arnhem Land	Central Australia	Western Desert		
G$_A$	10%	20%	11%	39%	41%	15%	15%
G$_B$	8%	2%	2%	0%	0%	13%	15%
G$_O$	82%	78%	87%	61%	59%	72%	70%

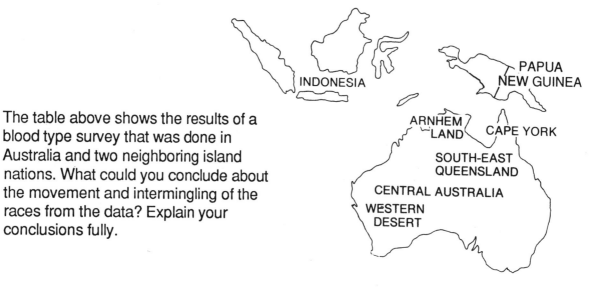

The table above shows the results of a blood type survey that was done in Australia and two neighboring island nations. What could you conclude about the movement and intermingling of the races from the data? Explain your conclusions fully.

Investigation Three

Inherited Diseases

An inherited disorder that causes great suffering is Huntington's chorea, also known as Huntington's disease. The disease usually develops between the ages of 35 and 45. With this disease, the central nervous system gradually degenerates, leading to death. There is no cure at this time. The condition is genetically dominant. The box at the right lists other health conditions that are genetically dominant.

1 a The famous folksinger Woody Guthrie died from Huntington's disease. He had several children, including a son, Arlo.
   i   Complete the gene table for Arlo's parents.
   ii What is the probability that Arlo has Huntington's disease?

Examples of Genetically Dominant Conditions
Achondroplasia
Dystrophia myotonica
Ehlers-Danlos syndrome
Huntington's chorea
Marfan's syndrome
Multiple exostoses
Multiple neurofibromatosis
Multiple polyposis of colon
Multiple telangiectasia
Myotonia congenita
Osteogensis imperfecta
Peutz's syndrome (spots)
Tuberous sclerosis

Woody Guthrie

	G_H	G_h
Arlo's mother G_h		
G_h		

G_H = gene for Huntington's chorea
G_h = gene for *not* having the disease

b When Clara is about to marry Patrick, she learns that her father has Huntington's disease. She reads in the paper that a test to determine whether or not she will develop the disease is now available. Clara wants to know if she is likely to give her and Patrick's children Huntington's chorea. If *you* were in Clara's position, would you take the test? Explain your reasoning.

c Suppose Clara does not take the test and instead takes the risk of having children who will develop Huntington's chorea. Complete these gene tables for Clara's children. Assume that Patrick does not carry the G_H gene.

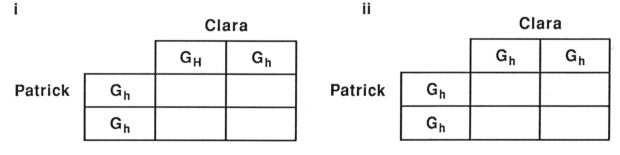

d Find the probability that any one of Clara's children will develop Huntington's disease.

e When she is 27 years old, Clara has a baby named Brenda. When Brenda is 16, her mother is diagnosed as having Huntington's chorea. What *now* is the probability that Brenda will eventually get the disease?

ON YOUR OWN

Suppose one of your first cousins develops Huntington's chorea. Draw family trees to help determine the probability you will get the disease.

2 Frances knows that her mother has Huntington's disease. She deduces that at least one of her maternal grandparents was a sufferer.

a Is her reasoning correct?

b Frances also deduces that at least one of her great-grandparents was a sufferer. Is she correct?

c Frances researches her family history for Huntington's disease.

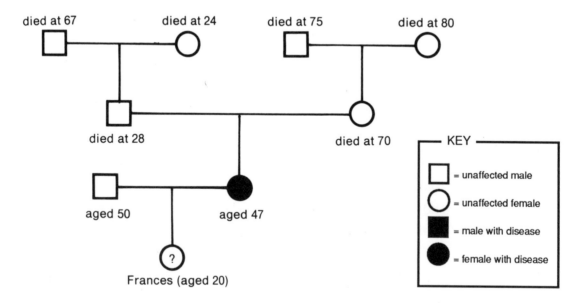

died at 67   died at 24   died at 75   died at 80

died at 28   died at 70

KEY
☐ = unaffected male
○ = unaffected female
■ = male with disease
● = female with disease

aged 50   aged 47

? Frances (aged 20)

Why doesn't Frances extend her father's tree?

d Her diagram does *not* show a grandparent or a great-grandparent with the disease. Does this mean her deductions in **a** and **b** are wrong? Explain your answer.

e In another family, Colin makes the family tree shown below. Who could yet develop Huntington's chorea in this family?

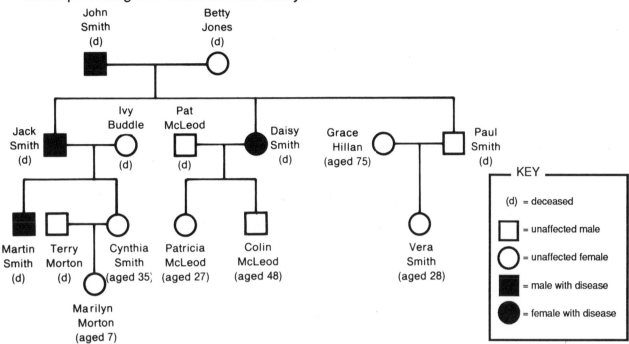

f In another family, Theresa's mother has Huntington's disease, but family members deny that either of Theresa's maternal grandparents had the disease. Give possible explanations for this denial.

3 Phenylketonuria (PKU) is an inherited recessive condition that is now routinely tested for at birth. One baby in 15 000 is affected. If untreated, the baby will develop brain damage. Other recessive conditions are listed in the box at the right.

a Find out about the treatment for PKU babies.

b Suppose that two parents, neither of whom suffer from PKU, have a PKU baby. Draw a gene diagram to explain how this could happen.

> G_p = gene for PKU — recessive
> G_P = gene for *not* carrying PKU — dominant

c Among Caucasians (whites), 1 person in 80 is a carrier of the gene for PKU. Given this data, explain why white PKU babies are rare.

Examples of Recessive Conditions

Amaurotic family idiocy
Congenital adrenal
   hyperplasia
Congenital microcytosis
Cystic fibrosis of the pancreas
Epidermolysis bullosa
   dystrophica (severe forms)
Galactoseamia
Glycogen storage disease
   (all types)
Infantile progressive
   muscular atrophy
Juvenile progressive
   muscular atrophy
Metachromatic leucodystrophy
Morquio's disease
Phenylketonuria
Sickle-cell anemia

---

4   Sickle-cell anemia is a blood disease that a child inherits from parents who are carriers. The recessive gene for sickle-cell anemia is carried by 1 in 10 Black Americans.

   a   Explain how sickle-cell anemia is inherited from carrier parents.

   b   A biologist estimates that 1 out of 400 babies with Black American parents will inherit sickle-cell anemia. How does she make this estimate?

5   Suppose a new disease is created by the *mutation* of a gene on a chromosome, and this mutated gene is recessive. This mutation occurs on a remote island that has been settled by only two couples, the Swansons and the McGills. Mr. McGill (unknown to himself) has this mutated gene. Later, scientists name the disease after him, saying that an affected person has McGill's disease. No one else is allowed to come to the island. The Swansons have four children (A, B, C, and D in the diagram below) who marry McGill children.

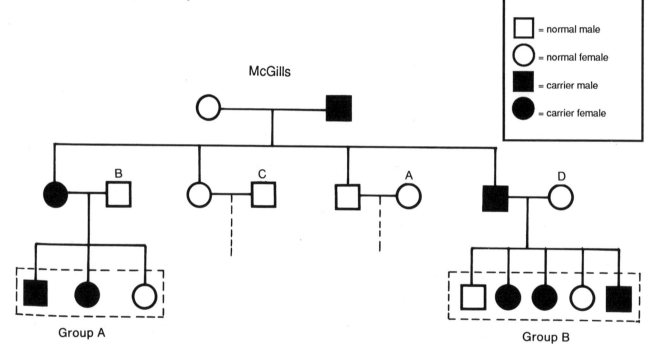

   a   Copy and extend the diagram to show how some people can inherit McGill's disease. (Intermarry the people in groups A and B).

   b   What warning about marrying close relatives does this illustrate?

   c   Investigate the prohibitions about marrying near relatives in various cultures.

   d   Two hundred years ago in the United States, three couples started a community now called the Old Order Amish. All subsequent marriages were between members of the order only. Since the start, there have been at least 61 cases of six-fingered dwarf children. This characteristic is recessive. Explain how the Amish community could, in the future, reduce the risk of producing more six-fingered dwarf children.

Investigation Four

Gender-Linked Diseases

Recall that most normal human cells have 46 chromosomes linked in pairs. Pairs 1 through 22 (44 chromosomes in all) are found in both males and females. The last pair, which determines gender, is special.

Every female has XX chromosomes and every male has XY chromosomes for the last pair. Notice that the Y chromosome is much smaller than the X chromosome, and so has very few genes. This fact explains why certain diseases can be inherited by boys but virtually never by girls.

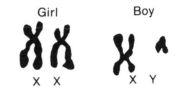

Girl   Boy

X   X   X   Y

The box at the right contains a list of X-linked health conditions.

> **Examples of X-Linked Conditions**
>
> Hemophilia
> Christmas disease
> Duchenne muscular dystrophy
> Glucose-6-phosphate dehydrogenase deficiency
> Nephrogenic diabetes insipidus

1 Hemophilia is a condition found almost exclusively in males. It is a recessive condition carried on the X chromosome, causing the sufferer to bleed endlessly from cuts because the blood fails to clot. The Y chromosome is small and has no blood-clotting gene.

> X_h = gene on the X chromosome *without* the clotting factor — recessive
>
> X_H = gene on the X chromosome *with* the clotting factor — dominant

a A person with an $X_h X_H$ gene pair is a female *carrier* of hemophilia who does not herself have the disease. Explain why.

b Write statements like the one in **a** for each of the following gene pairs:
  i $X_H X_H$ **ii** $X_H Y$ **iii** $X_h Y$

c In the past, a person with $X_h Y$ seldom reached adulthood. Why do you suppose this was the case?

d Suppose a hemophiliac male ($X_h Y$) survives to adulthood. He marries a non-carrier female ($X_H X_H$).
  i Draw a table showing the possible combinations of the gender chromosomes for their children.

   ii Prove that their sons are *never* hemophiliacs.

   iii Prove that their daughters are *always* carriers.

e Suppose a hemophiliac male (X_hY) survives to adulthood but, unknown to them both, he marries a carrier female (X_hX_H). Show how they can have a hemophiliac daughter. (Although this situation is rare, at least two cases of hemophiliac girls have been observed in Britain.)

2 This family tree shows details of the royal families of Europe.

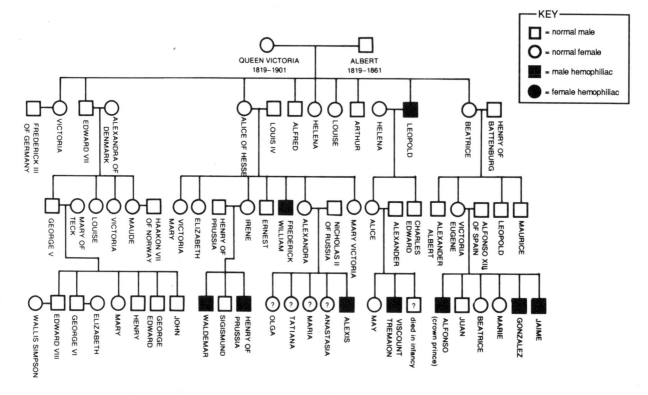

a Study the tree carefully to explain which of the following statements are true.

   i   Queen Victoria was a carrier of hemophilia.

   ii   No hemophiliac in the tree survived long enough to have children.

   iii Alice of Hesse was a carrier.

   iv Alexandra of Denmark was not a carrier.

   v   Beatrice was a carrier, and so was Victoria Eugenie.

   vi Alexandra (who married Tsar Nicholas II of Russia) was not a carrier.

   vii Victoria Mary, who was the daughter of Alice of Hesse and the grandmother of Prince Philip, Duke of Edinburgh, was a carrier.

   viii The British royal line—Victoria, Edward VII, George V, George VI, and, (not shown) Elizabeth II, the future Charles III, and the future William IV —is now probably free of hemophilia.

b Why do you suppose Olga, Tatiana, Maria, and Anastasia Romanov have question marks in their circles? (A history book may help you on this one.)

3 Ron and Marian have a colorblind son named Andrew. A biologist tells them that colorblindness is gender-linked and recessive. (The Y chromosome carries no genes for vision.)

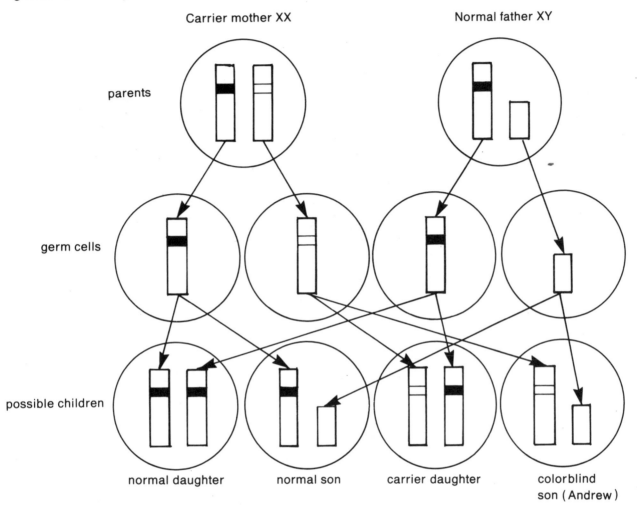

Carrier mother XX   Normal father XY

parents

germ cells

possible children

normal daughter   normal son   carrier daughter   colorblind son (Andrew)

Marian's parents are named Dorothy and Fletcher. Fletcher is not colorblind.

a Draw a diagram like the one shown here, placing Dorothy and Fletcher at the top. Indicate Marian on the diagram.

b Andrew marries Heather, who is not colorblind. To their surprise, they have a colorblind daughter, Lisa. Draw another diagram that would help to explain this fact, placing Andrew and Heather at the top.

c Could Andrew and Heather have a son with normal sight?

d Their second child is a son. What is the probability that he is colorblind?

CHECK-UP

1   Sue and Neil both have straight noses. Their child, Emily, has a concave nose.

   a   Does this show that the concave-nose gene is recessive or dominant?

   b   If Emily marries a male with a concave nose, is it possible that their child will have a straight nose? Explain your answer.

2   Rafael has blood type O and his sister has type AB. What are the blood types of their parents?

3   Lamont and Stacey (who are married) both have brown eyes, as do both sets of parents. Their son has blue eyes. Is this possible? Explain your answer.

4   Curly hair is a dominant gene, G_H. Straight hair is the recessive gene, G_h. Ian's mother has straight hair, but Ian has curly hair. Jill's mother has straight hair, but Jill has curly hair. Use a diagram to show that Ian and Jill's children have a 25 percent chance of having straight hair.

5   Cystic fibrosis is a chronic genetic disorder that affects the pancreas, the lungs, or both, and is usually fatal in childhood. One in 25 Caucasians carries this defective gene.

   a   Is this gene recessive or dominant? Explain your answer.

   b   Show that the probability that two Caucasians will have a child with cystic fibrosis is 1 in 2500.

   c   Given a couple who have one child with the disease, what is the probability of their having another child who has the disease?

6   There are 1484 dominant disorders and 1117 recessive disorders. However, *deadly* dominant disorders are rare.

   a   Why do you suppose this is so?

   b   Find an example of a dominant condition that is deadly and explain why it has continued to exist.

7   Suppose that Dr. Lum discovers an X-linked disease that is recessive and deadly in childhood. It is called Lum's syndrome after the discoverer.

   a   Explain why girls would *never* get Lum's syndrome.

   b   i   Draw a diagram showing how a boy could inherit Lum's syndrome.
       ii If Rick's mother is a carrier of Lum's syndrome, what is the probability Rick will develop the disease?

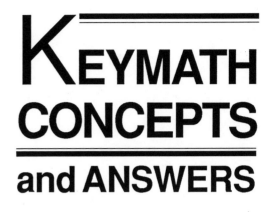

KEYMATH CONCEPTS

These KEYMATH activities can help you understand the math concepts you may need as you do the investigations. In the margins of the investigations, you sometimes see a little key. The number in the key identifies which KEYMATH activity you might want to review. Answers to the KEYMATH activities are given at the end of this section.

1

To round to a particular decimal place, look at the digit immediately to the right of that place. If it is 5 or larger, increase the rounded digit to the next higher value; if it is *less* than 5, do not change the rounded digit. Then drop any digits after the one you have rounded. For example, 2.467 rounded to the nearest tenth is 2.5.

Sometimes rounding is stated in terms of *significant digits*. A digit in a number is significant unless it is a zero whose only purpose is to help place the decimal point. That is, 0.05 has *one* significant digit (5) since the two zeros are included only to help place the decimal point properly; whereas 0.0600 has three significant digits (600). All non-zero digits in a number are significant. Thus, 435.62 has *five* significant digits. Zeros between two non-zero digits are also significant. Thus, 205.4 has *four* significant digits. Rounding 0.1448 to two significant digits gives you 0.15.

a Round 0.0800 to
   i one decimal place.
   ii two significant digits.

b Round the numbers in the tables as indicated.

   i

Number	Number of Decimal Places	Rounded Number
86.0908	1	
86.0908	2	
86.0908	3	
0.004906	3	
0.004906	4	
0.004906	5	

   ii

Number	Number of Significant Figures	Rounded Number
174.0904	4	
174.0904	3	
174.0904	2	
0.06090	1	
0.06090	2	
0.06090	3	

2

When you are multiplying or dividing values that involve measures (length, weight, area, and so on), here's a good rule of thumb: Write the answer using *no more* significant digits than the *least* number of significant digits found in any of the numbers you used in the calculation. For example, it is sensible to write $3.5 \times 0.346 \approx 1.2$, since 3.5 has only two significant digits. (The symbol $\approx$ means *approximately equal to.*)

a Why is $8.900 \text{ m} \times 7.37 \text{ m} \approx 65.6 \text{ m}^2$ a sensible answer?

b Give sensible answers for the following:

i	$10.9 \text{ m} \times 14.71 \text{ m}$	**vii**	$291 \text{ km} \div 17 \text{ h}$
ii	$16.88 \text{ km} \times 3.74 \text{ km}$	**viii**	$381.4 \text{ km} \div 7.26 \text{ h}$
iii	$188.8 \text{ cm}^2 \times 3.81 \text{ cm}$	**ix**	$66.24 \text{ m}^2 \div 11.88 \text{ m}$
iv	$10.8 \text{ km/h} \times 36.81 \text{ h}$	**x**	$8804 \text{ cm}^2 \div 1.4 \text{ cm}$
v	$0.0912 \text{ h/km} \times 14 \text{ km}$	**xi**	$861.3 \text{ cm} \div 11.8 \text{ s}$
vi	$808 \text{ cm} \times 414 \text{ cm}$	**xii**	$441 \text{ m} \div 48.21 \text{ s}$

3

When you are multiplying or dividing three or more numbers, avoid rounding intermediate answers, because this generally leads to inaccurate answers.

a Show that $1.93 \times 6.36 \times 0.964 = 11.832\,907\,2$ (exactly).

b Show that $1.93 \times 6.36 \approx 12.3$ (rounded sensibly), and then $12.3 \times 0.964 = 11.857\,2$ (exactly).

c Explain why the two-step exercise in **b** gives an answer different from that in **a**, even though the same numbers are being multiplied.

d Repeat **a**, **b**, and **c** with a problem you make up yourself.

4

When you are solving problems that involve money, "sensible rounding" usually means rounding to the nearest cent or the nearest dollar. You generally would not use the significant-digit rounding rule, because you always want your answer to be in the form $XX or $XX.XX.

a Jenny pays $84.38 for 7 plates. Show that the cost of 1 plate is $12.05, rounded sensibly.

b Vince buys an 11-acre piece of property for $105 500. Show that an average cost of $9590 per acre is a sensibly rounded answer. Is $9600 a reasonable answer for some situations?

5

If $ax + b = c$, then $x = \dfrac{c - b}{a}$. If $a + bx = c$, then $x = \dfrac{c - a}{b}$

For example, if $5x + 4 = 15$, then $x = \dfrac{15 - 4}{5} = 2.2$

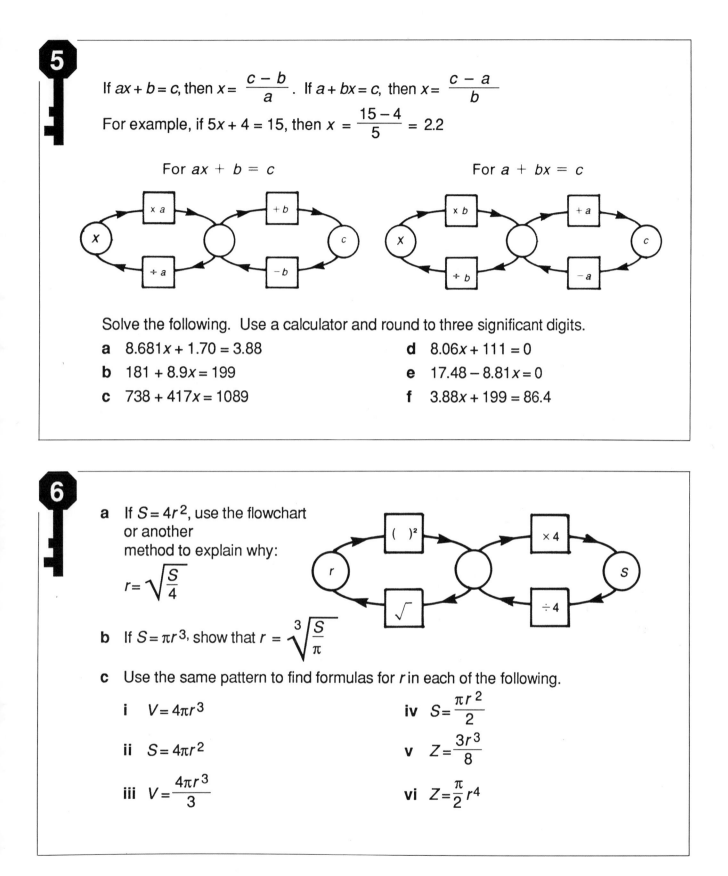

For $ax + b = c$

For $a + bx = c$

Solve the following. Use a calculator and round to three significant digits.

a $8.681x + 1.70 = 3.88$

b $181 + 8.9x = 199$

c $738 + 417x = 1089$

d $8.06x + 111 = 0$

e $17.48 - 8.81x = 0$

f $3.88x + 199 = 86.4$

6

a If $S = 4r^2$, use the flowchart or another method to explain why:
$r = \sqrt{\dfrac{S}{4}}$

b If $S = \pi r^3$, show that $r = \sqrt[3]{\dfrac{S}{\pi}}$

c Use the same pattern to find formulas for r in each of the following.

i $V = 4\pi r^3$

ii $S = 4\pi r^2$

iii $V = \dfrac{4\pi r^3}{3}$

iv $S = \dfrac{\pi r^2}{2}$

v $Z = \dfrac{3r^3}{8}$

vi $Z = \dfrac{\pi}{2} r^4$

7

For a car traveling a distance d, at average speed s, for a time t,
then $d = s \times t$.

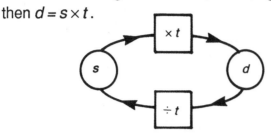
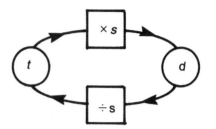

a Compute the missing values in the tables. (Round sensibly.)

i

d (m)	t (s)	s (m/s)
186	36	
334	11	
	20.6	12
40.5		20.1
	30.8	18.3

ii

d (km)	t (h)	s (km/h)
320.6	4.11	
480.8	8.07	
	4.0	40.66
300.4		100.62
	3.47	50.0

8

A car that consumes gasoline
at a rate of r miles per gallon
uses g gallons of gasoline.
The distance d that it travels
is found using the formula
$d = g \times r$.

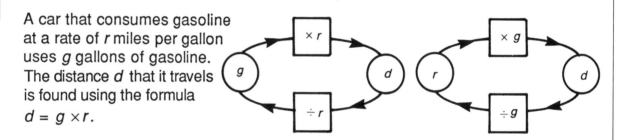

a A car travels 8061 miles. Its rate of gasoline consumption is 19.5 miles/gallon. Show that it uses about 413 gallons of gasoline for this trip.

b A car travels 2356 miles. Its rate of gasoline consumption is 32 miles/gallon. How many gallons of gasoline does the car use for this trip?

c Compute the missing values in the tables. (Round sensibly.)

i

d (mi)	g (gal)	r (mi/gal)
861	41.8	
76.8	3.6	
8688	339.3	
17408		29.6
	41.2	22.7

ii

d (mi)	g (gal)	r (mi/gal)
29681	1481	
	481.3	14.6
763.9		19.9
	81.7	24.5
	79.7	35.0

9

For a circle of radius *r*, diameter *d*, and circumference *C*,

$C = 2\pi r = \pi d$ (where $\pi \approx 3.1415927$)

$d = 2r$

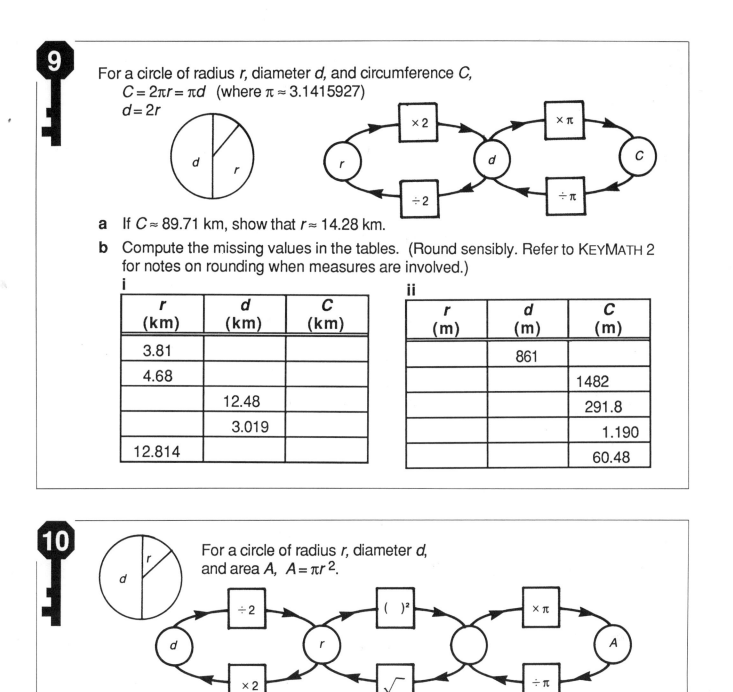

a If $C \approx 89.71$ km, show that $r \approx 14.28$ km.

b Compute the missing values in the tables. (Round sensibly. Refer to KEYMATH 2 for notes on rounding when measures are involved.)

i

r (km)	*d* (km)	*C* (km)
3.81		
4.68		
	12.48	
	3.019	
12.814		

ii

r (m)	*d* (m)	*C* (m)
	861	
		1482
		291.8
		1.190
		60.48

10

For a circle of radius *r*, diameter *d*, and area *A*, $A = \pi r^2$.

a If $A \approx 381$ cm², show that $d \approx 22.0$ cm.

b Find the missing values in the tables. (Round sensibly.)

i

r (mm)	*d* (mm)	*A* (mm²)
81		
40.9		
	126.6	
	300.4	

ii

r (cm)	*d* (cm)	*A* (cm²)
		844
		89.91
		63.418
		4089

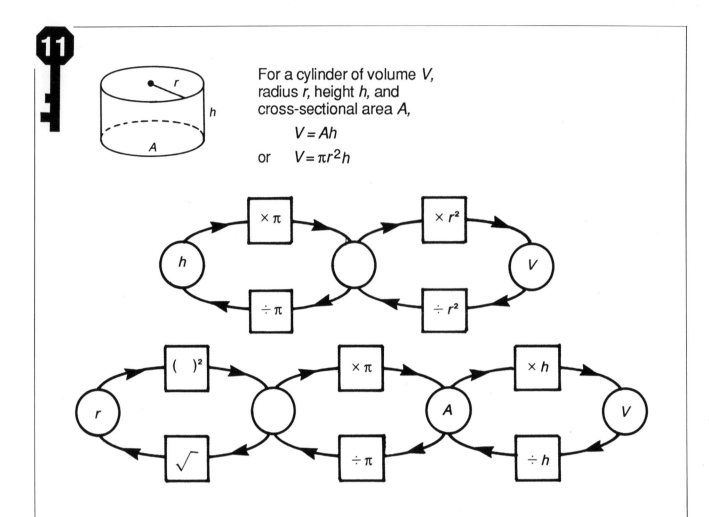

For a cylinder of volume V, radius r, height h, and cross-sectional area A,

$$V = Ah$$
or $$V = \pi r^2 h$$

a i If $V \approx 375$ ml (375 cm³) and $r \approx 2.91$ cm, show that $h \approx 14.1$ cm is a sensible answer.

ii If $V \approx 451$ ml (451 cm³) and $h \approx 8.96$ cm, show that $r \approx 4.00$ cm is a sensible answer.

b Compute the missing values in the tables. (Round sensibly.)

i

h (mm)	r (mm)	V (mm³)
6.8	4.9	
34.8	21.3	
761	86.3	
	11.4	998.8

ii

h (cm)	r (cm)	V (cm³)
	19.6	2041
	24.6	2840
11.3		846.1
17.44		779.2

12

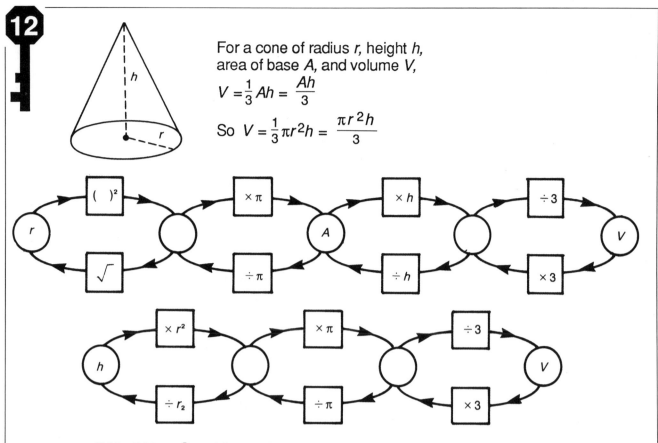

For a cone of radius r, height h, area of base A, and volume V,

$$V = \frac{1}{3}Ah = \frac{Ah}{3}$$

So $V = \frac{1}{3}\pi r^2 h = \frac{\pi r^2 h}{3}$

a If $V \approx 833$ cm³ and $h \approx 14.8$ cm, show that $r \approx 7.33$ cm is a sensible answer.

b Compute the missing values in the tables. (Round sensibly.)

i

h (cm)	r (cm)	V (cm³)
16.3	14.7	
28	13	
81.31	41.06	
	23.8	9014

ii

h (mm)	r (mm)	V (mm³)
	108.4	98143
61.4		8439
71.4		780639
22		777.8

13

To find 15% of a price P, you multiply the decimal/percent equivalent by the price in dollars and cents: $0.15 \times P$

Find the following percents. (Round sensibly.)

a 18% of $9.30   c 36% of $1440   e 6% of $3.91

b 4.1% of $801   d 86% of $11.37   f 14.8% of $41.41

14

a Percent means *per hundred*. To express a decimal number as a percent, multiply the decimal by 100 — or simply move the decimal point two places to the right. For example, 1.32 = 132%. Use a calculator to help explain why $16.3 \div 91.4 \approx 0.178 = 17.8\%$.

b Use a calculator to do the following exercises, then express each decimal answer as a percent. (Round sensibly.)

i $17.8\% \div 28.8 \approx 0.\underline{\quad} = \underline{\quad}\%$

ii $86 \div 901 \approx 0.\underline{\quad} = \underline{\quad}\%$

iii $0.871 \div 0.978 \approx 0.\underline{\quad} = \underline{\quad}\%$

iv $1.53 \div 39.87 \approx 0.\underline{\quad} = \underline{\quad}\%$

v $0.0481 \div 0.937 \approx 0.\underline{\quad} = \underline{\quad}\%$

vi $381 \div 4884 \approx 0.\underline{\quad} = \underline{\quad}\%$

vii 22 out of 35 $\approx 0.\underline{\quad} = \underline{\quad}\%$

viii 18 out of 29 $\approx 0.\underline{\quad} = \underline{\quad}\%$

15

Suppose you want to add on a certain percentage—say 15%—to a cost price *CP*, to find the selling price *SP*. This can be done in two ways.

Method A

$SP = (15\% \times CP) + CP$

$\quad\; = (0.15 \times CP) + CP$

Method B

$SP = 115\% \times CP$

$\quad\; = 1.15 \times CP$

The flowchart is based on Method B, for a markup of *r*%.

a A retailer marks up a radio by 35% and sells it for $319. Show that $CP \approx \$236$ is a sensible answer.

b Compute the missing values in the tables. (Round to the nearest dollar).

i

CP ($)	Markup	SP ($)
914	31%	
741	28%	
13406	81%	
	42%	41 231

ii

CP ($)	Markup	SP ($)
	70%	55
	21%	882
2811	−28%	
419		713

    MATHEMATICAL INVESTIGATIONS • DALE SEYMOUR PUBLICATIONS

16

Suppose you want to subtract a certain percentage, say 18%, from a usual price UP to find the discount price DP. This can be done in two ways.

Method A

$$DP = UP - (18\% \times UP)$$
$$= UP - (0.18 \times UP)$$

Method B

$$DP = 82\% \times UP$$
$$= 0.82 \times UP$$

The flowchart is based on Method B, for a reduction of $r\%$.

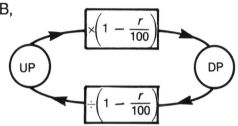

a A retailer discounts a $48 shirt by 30%. Show that $DP \approx \$34$ is a sensible answer.

b Compute the missing values in the tables. (Round to the nearest dollar.)

i

UP ($)	Discount	DP ($)
804	41%	
9141	7%	
487	19%	
	26%	3091

ii

UP ($)	Discount	DP ($)
	21%	788
	47%	10814
91	4%	
814	14%	

17

If a price increases first by $r_1\%$, then by another $r_2\%$, the total increase is *not* $(r_1 + r_2)\%$.

a A bicycle that used to cost $289.50 has increased in price by 8.3% Show that the new price is $313.53.

b The price of the bicycle in **a** is raised further by 17.6%. Show that the price is now $368.71.

c The sum of the two rate increases is 8.3% + 17.6% = 25.9%. Demonstrate that simply increasing the original price of $289.50 by 25.9% does not give the correct answer shown in **b**. Explain why.

d Repeat **a**, **b**, and **c** with a problem you make up yourself.

18

For a triangle of base b, height h, and area A,

$$A = \frac{1}{2}bh$$

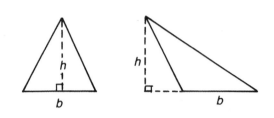

a If $A = 60$ cm^2 and $h = 10$ cm, show that $b = 12$ cm.

b Compute the missing values in the tables. (Rounding is not required.)

i

b (mm)	h (mm)	A (mm^2)
70	80	
100	60	
110	80	
140	100	

ii

b (cm)	h (cm)	A (cm^2)
16		80
	20	100
40		200
	200	10000

19

For a rectangle of length x, width y, area A, and perimeter P,

$$A = xy$$
$$P = 2(x + y) = 2x + 2y$$

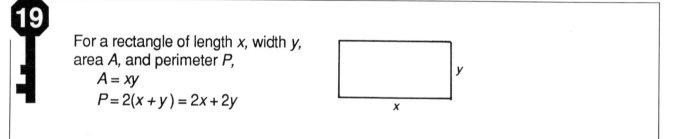

a If $A = 60$ cm^2 and $x = 6$ cm, show that $P = 32$ cm.

b Compute the missing values in the tables. (Round to the nearest whole number.)

i

x (cm)	y (cm)	P (cm)	A (cm^2)
6	8		
10	14		
8	12		
10			80
	8		160

ii

x (cm)	y (cm)	P (cm)	A (cm^2)
4	5		
9			81
	7	26	
	10	34	
		22	30

20

For a cuboid with sides *x, y,* and *z,* total surface area *T,* and volume *V:*

area of front face = xy
area of side face = yz
area of bottom face = xz
$T = 2xy + 2yz + 2xz = 2(xy + yz + xz)$
$V = xyz$

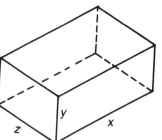

a If $x \approx 13.8$, $y \approx 14.9$ cm, $z \approx 20.8$ cm, show that $T \approx 1610$ cm² is a sensible answer.

b Compute the missing values in the table.

x (cm)	y (cm)	z (cm)	2xy (cm²)	2yz (cm²)	2xz (cm²)	T (cm²)	V (cm³)
18.4	20.31	24.6					
181.8	204.3	86.4					
8.44	9.38	23.86					
174	288	83.1					
1.093	2.143	2.880					
0.921	0.921	0.921					

c If $x \approx 12.8$ cm, $y \approx 15.3$ cm, and $T \approx 1584$ cm², find *z.*

d For a cube with side *x,* show that $T = 6x^2$.

21

Here are two ways to find the area of a polygonal figure. The method you choose in any given case may depend on the shape of the polygon.

Method A
Inscribe the polygon (E) in a rectangle. Find the area of each of the figures that surround the polygon (in the diagram, triangles A, B, C, and D). Add those areas and subtract the total from the area of the entire rectangle to find the area of polygon E.

Method B
Draw lines to divide the polygonal figure into triangular and rectangular shapes (in the diagram, triangles F, H, and I and rectangle G). Find the area of each of these smaller figures and total them to find the area of the entire polygon.

a Find the area of
i A   **ii** B   **iii** C   **iv** D
(See KEYMATH 18, if necessary, for notes on finding the area of a triangle.)

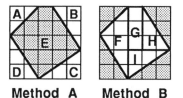

Method A   Method B

b Find the area of E using your answers in **a.**

c Use the second diagram and Method B to find the area of polygon E.

22

a If a batter scores *n* runs in *x* innings at an average of *a* runs per inning, explain why *n* = a*x*.

b **i** Kevin averages 0.68 runs per inning in 47 innings. What is his total number of runs?

   ii The next season, Kevin averages 0.74 runs in 27 innings. What is his total number of runs this season?

   iii Show that his average over the two seasons is 0.70.

c Compute the missing values in the table.

First Season			Second Season			Average Over Two Seasons
Runs	Innings Completed	Average	Runs	Innings Completed	Average	
	13	0.15		18	0.61	
	26	0.38		8	0.38	
	41	0.20	13		0.72	
5	12		8		0.53	

23

A car moves *d* feet in *t* seconds.

a Using the data in this chart, show that the car moves 5 feet in the third second and that its average speed at that point is 5 ft/s.

t	*d*
0	0
1	3
2	7
3	12
4	14
5	15

Start Time (s)	Finish Time (s)	Average Speed (ft/s)
0	5	
1	4	
2	4	
2	5	
3	5	
4	5	

b Show that the average speed in the fourth second is 2 ft/s.

c Show that the average speed from *t* = 1 to *t* = 5 is 3 ft/s.

d Use the data in the chart to compute the missing values in the table.

24

For a right triangle with sides a, b, and c,

$$a^2 = b^2 + c^2$$
$$b^2 = a^2 - c^2$$
$$c^2 = a^2 - b^2$$

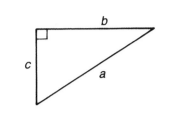

a If $a \approx 11.6$ cm and $b = 8.6$ cm, show that $c \approx 7.8$ cm.

b Compute the missing values in the tables. (Round to one decimal place.)

i

b (m)	c (m)	a (m)
14.9	12.6	
50.3	60.7	
1.7	3.8	
4.2		5.9
	3.9	6.9

ii

b (cm)	c (cm)	a (cm)
261.8	268.7	
	274.4	401.9
	407.9	581.3
281.8	384.7	
	46.9	46.0

25

Shown here is a rough sketch of △ABC. Use a compass and a ruler to make an accurate drawing of △ABC as described below.

a Draw a line segment $\overline{YX}$.

b Construct a line segment $\overline{BC}$ 35 mm long at right angles to $\overline{YX}$.

c Set the compass for a radius of 50 mm and, using B as the center, make an arc at A. Draw line segment $\overline{AB}$.

d Show that the following are true by measuring with a ruler and protractor:

  i $\overline{AC} \approx 36$ mm

  ii $\alpha \approx 44°$

Repeat the steps above to draw five more triangles, using the values in the table.

BC (mm)	AB (mm)	AC (mm)	α
35	50	36	44°
25	70		
35	65		
41	49		
53	68		

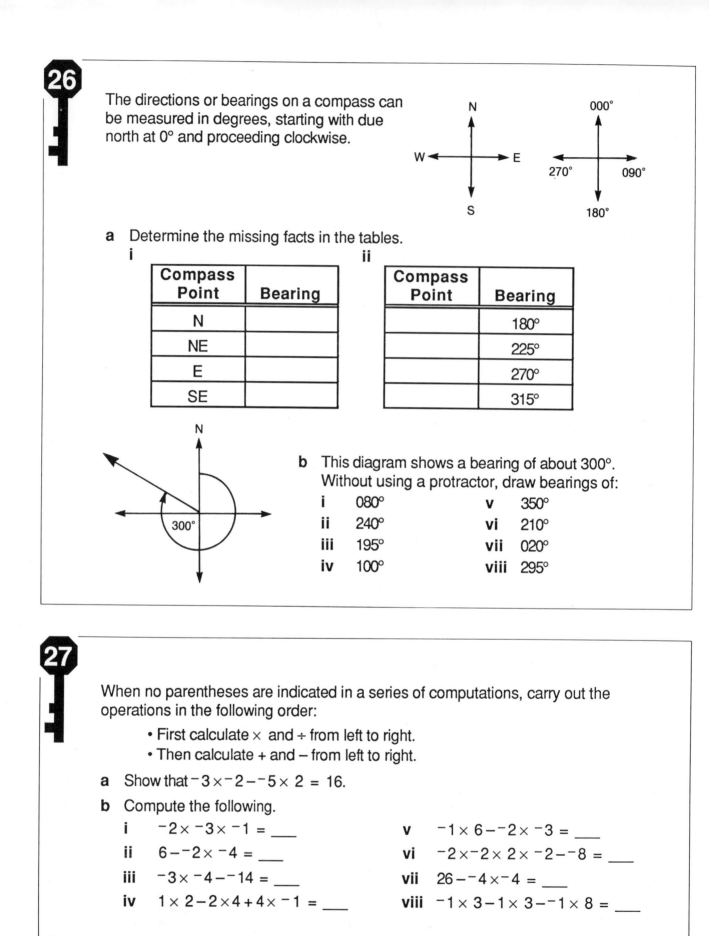

26

The directions or bearings on a compass can be measured in degrees, starting with due north at 0° and proceeding clockwise.

a Determine the missing facts in the tables.

i

Compass Point	Bearing
N	
NE	
E	
SE	

ii

Compass Point	Bearing
	180°
	225°
	270°
	315°

b This diagram shows a bearing of about 300°. Without using a protractor, draw bearings of:

i	080°	**v**	350°
ii	240°	**vi**	210°
iii	195°	**vii**	020°
iv	100°	**viii**	295°

27

When no parentheses are indicated in a series of computations, carry out the operations in the following order:

- First calculate × and ÷ from left to right.
- Then calculate + and − from left to right.

a Show that $^-3 \times ^-2 - ^-5 \times 2 = 16$.

b Compute the following.

i $^-2 \times ^-3 \times ^-1 =$ ___

ii $6 - ^-2 \times ^-4 =$ ___

iii $^-3 \times ^-4 - ^-14 =$ ___

iv $1 \times 2 - 2 \times 4 + 4 \times ^-1 =$ ___

v $^-1 \times 6 - ^-2 \times ^-3 =$ ___

vi $^-2 \times ^-2 \times 2 \times ^-2 - ^-8 =$ ___

vii $26 - ^-4 \times ^-4 =$ ___

viii $^-1 \times 3 - 1 \times 3 - ^-1 \times 8 =$ ___

28

In the expression 3^4, the value 3 is called the *base* and 4 is called the *exponent*. The expression $3^4 = 3 \times 3 \times 3 \times 3 = 81$.

Complete the following equations.

a $16 = 2^{\square}$

b $8 = 2^{\square}$

c $4 = 2^{\square}$

d $2 = 2^{\square}$

e $1 = 2^{\square}$

f $2^6 =$ ___

g $2^8 =$ ___

h $3^4 =$ ___

i $10^3 =$ ___

j $5^3 =$ ___

k $8^2 =$ ___

l $8^0 =$ ___

29

The following are examples of the *distributive* property of multiplication over addition and multiplication over subtraction:

$$a(b + c) = ab + ac$$
and $$(a + b)c = ac + bc$$

$$a(b - c) = ab - ac$$
and $$(a - b)c = ac - bc$$

a   Explain why $2x(3x - 4) = 6x^2 - 8x$.

b   Expand each of the following expressions.

   i $3x(4x + 3) =$

   ii $2x(1 - 2x) =$

   iii $x(3 - 4x) =$

   iv $(3y + 1)y =$

   v $(4y + 3)y =$

   vi $2y(7 - 3y) =$

   vii $(y + 7)y =$

   viii $(3f - 1)f =$

30

If two equations have one variable in common, it is generally possible to reduce the two expressions to a single equation by substitution.

a If $z = xy$ and $y = 2x^2$, explain why $z = 2x^3$. (Note that the y has been eliminated.)

b Reduce each of the following pairs to a single equation by eliminating the y variable.

   i $z = yx^2$ and $y = 3x$ **iv** $y = 4r$ and $z = 2r^2y^2$

   ii $z = y^2x$ and $y = x$ **v** $y = \frac{1}{2}x$ and $z = 8x^2y$

   iii $z = y^2x^2$ and $y = 2x$ **vi** $y = \frac{x}{2}$ and $z = 8xy^2$

31

When you have a two-column table, you can often find a general rule, or *formula,* that relates all pairs of values in the table. Information that is provided in the problem statement may help you discover the formula.

a Jill orders x shirts at \$15 each from a mail order house. Postage and handling is \$4 for any order. She pays a total of C. Complete this table relating the number and cost of shirts.

x	C ($\$$)	Pattern
1	19	
2	34	$(2 \times 15) + 4$
3		
4		
5		

b Determine the formula for this table. (*Hint:* $C = \square x + \triangle$)

c Find a formula for each of the following tables.

i

x	C
1	5
2	9
3	13
4	17

ii

x	C
1	7
2	10
3	13
4	16

iii

x	C
1	9
2	14
3	19
4	24

32

If you buy three times as much of something, you would generally expect to pay three times the price. For example, suppose 2 loaves of bread cost $1.50. To buy 6 loaves, you would have to spend 3 times as much, or $4.50. The ratio of the new amount (6) to the old amount (2) is $\frac{6}{2} = 3$. We call this number the *scale factor*. We can use it to determine cost.

a Jack pays $12.50 for a 1.65 m length of material. Joan buys 2.85 m of the same material and wants to know its cost.

Use a calculator to show that the number missing from the scale factor box in the flowchart must be 1.727 272 7.

b Use **a** to show that Joan will pay $21.59 for her material.

c Use a calculator to compute the missing values in the following table.

Length of Material A (m)	Cost of Length A ($)	Length of Material B (m)	Scale Factor (unrounded)	Cost of Length B ($)
1.65	12.50	2.85	1.727 272 7	21.59
3.50	36.40	5.50		
4.25	89.20	26.50		
12.50	114.50	14.50		
3.75	36.75	2.25		
7.50	91.25	3.50		

33

Equations of the form $x = ay + b$ have several pairs of numbers (x,y) that make the equation true. If you graph these pairs of (x,y) values as points on a coordinate plane, their graph will be a straight line. For example, consider the following points for the equation $x = 3y - 1$:

$$(2, 1) \rightarrow 2 = 3 \times 1 - 1$$
$$(5, 2) \rightarrow 5 = 3 \times 2 - 1$$
$$(8, 3) \rightarrow 8 = 3 \times 3 - 1$$

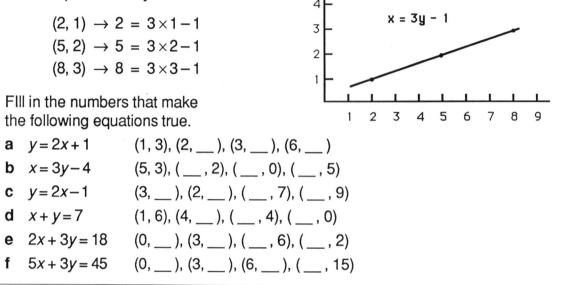

Fill in the numbers that make the following equations true.

a $y = 2x + 1$ $(1, 3), (2, \_\_), (3, \_\_), (6, \_\_)$

b $x = 3y - 4$ $(5, 3), (\_\_ , 2), (\_\_ , 0), (\_\_ , 5)$

c $y = 2x - 1$ $(3, \_\_), (2, \_\_), (\_\_ , 7), (\_\_ , 9)$

d $x + y = 7$ $(1, 6), (4, \_\_), (\_\_ , 4), (\_\_ , 0)$

e $2x + 3y = 18$ $(0, \_\_), (3, \_\_), (\_\_ , 6), (\_\_ , 2)$

f $5x + 3y = 45$ $(0, \_\_), (3, \_\_), (6, \_\_), (\_\_ , 15)$

34

The graph of an inequality of the form $ax + by \leq c$ or $ax + by \geq c$ fills half of the coordinate plane. To construct a graph of the inequality $x + y \leq 6$, we first graph the equality $x + y = 6$, then determine on which side of the line are the points that make the inequality true. In this example, the graph of $x + y \leq 6$ is shaded below the line because a point like $(0, 0)$ or $(1, 1)$ satisfies the inequality.

Note that the graph for any $\leq$ and $\geq$ inequality *includes the points on the line,* whereas the graph for any $<$ or $>$ inequality does *not* include the points on the line. For graphs of the latter type, use a dotted line to indicate that the line is not included in the graph, as shown in the second example.

Draw graphs of the following inequalities.

a $x + y < 6$

b $x + y \geq 6$

c $x - y \leq 8$

d $y > 2x - 4$

e $y \leq 2x - 4$

f $3x + 7y \leq 21$

g $x > 2y + 1$

h $3y + 2x \geq 12$

i $y - 2x \geq 8$

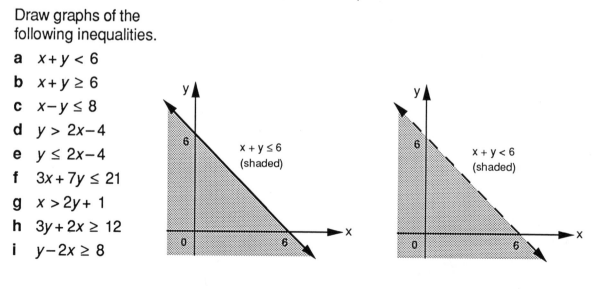

Figure A has *rotational symmetry* because we can rotate the rectangle less than a full turn about a point in the center square to a second position that exactly matches its starting position. Figure B has *line symmetry* because we can draw a vertical line through the center squares, and the rectangle, when flipped across that line, exactly matches its starting position.

Figure A

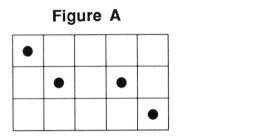

Figure B

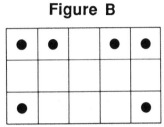

Make two copies of each of the following four figures. Add additional dots to each figure to give them the following properties:

i   rotational but *not* line symmetry.

ii line but *not* rotational symmetry.

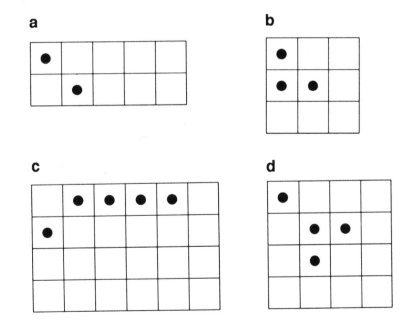

Answers

1 **a i** 0.1
  a ii 0.080
  b i 86.1, 86.09, 86.091, 0.005, 0.004 9,
  0.004 91
  b ii 174.1, 174, 170, 0.06, 0.061, 0.0609

2 **a** The number 8.900 has 4 significant figures
  and 7.37 has 3 significant figures. The product
  should have 3 significant figures.
  b i 160 m^2
  b ii 63.1 km^2
  b iii 719 cm^3
  b iv 398 km
  b v 1.3 h
  b vi 335 000 cm^2
  b vii 17 km/h
  b viii 52.5 km/h
  b ix 5.576 m
  b x 6 300 cm
  b xi 73.0 cm/s
  b xii 9.15 m/s

3 **c** The rounding in **b** was done too early.

4 **a** $84.38 ÷ 7 = $12.054285, or $12.05
  b Yes, when an approximate cost to the nearest
  $100 is sufficient.

5 **a** 0.251
  b 2.02
  c 0.842
  d −13.7
  e 1.98
  f −29.0

6 **c i** $r = \sqrt[3]{\dfrac{V}{4\pi}}$ **c ii** $r = \sqrt{\dfrac{S}{4\pi}}$

  c iii $r = \sqrt[3]{\dfrac{3V}{4\pi}}$ **c iv** $r = \sqrt{\dfrac{2S}{\pi}}$

  c v $r = \sqrt[3]{\dfrac{8Z}{3}}$ **c vi** $r = \sqrt[4]{\dfrac{2Z}{\pi}}$

7 **a i**

d (m)	t (s)	s (m/s)
186	36	**5.2**
334	11	**30**
250	20.6	12
40.5	**2.01**	20.1
564	30.8	18.3

a ii

d (km)	t (h)	s (km/h)
320.6	4.11	**78.0**
480.8	8.07	**59.6**
160	4.0	40.66
300.4	**2.985**	100.62
174	3.47	50.0

8 **a** 8061 ÷ 19.5 = 413.38, or about 413 gallons.
  b About 74 gallons.
  c i

d (mi)	g (gal)	r (mi/gal)
861	41.8	**20.6**
76.8	3.6	**21.3**
8688	339.3	**25.6**
17408	**588.1**	29.6
935	41.2	22.7

c ii

d (mi)	g (gal)	r (mi/gal)
29681	1481	**20.0**
7027	481.3	14.6
763.9	**38.4**	19.9
2002	81.7	24.5
2789.5	79.7	35.0

9 **a** r = 89.71 ÷ 2 (3.1416) = 14.277756, or 14.28
  (2 significant places)
  b i

r (km)	d (km)	C (km)
3.81	**7.62**	**23.9**
4.68	**9.36**	**29.4**
6.24	12.48	**39.21**
1.510	3.019	**9.484**
12.814	25.628	**80.513**

b ii

r (m)	d (m)	C (m)
431	861	**2700**
235.9	**471.7**	1482
46.44	92.88	291.8
0.1894	**0.3788**	1.190
9.626	**19.25**	60.48

10 a $r = \sqrt{\dfrac{381}{\pi}} = 11.0$, so $d = 22.0$

b i

r (mm)	d (mm)	A (mm^2)
81	**162**	**21000**
40.9	**81.8**	**5260**
63.3	126.6	**12590**
150.2	300.4	**70870**

b ii

r (cm)	d (cm)	A (cm^2)
16.4	**32.8**	844
5.350	**10.70**	89.91
4.4929	**8.9859**	63.418
36.08	**72.15**	4089

11 a i $h = \dfrac{375}{2.91^2} \div \pi \approx 14.1$ cm

a ii $r = \sqrt{\dfrac{451}{8.96} \div \pi} \approx 4.00$ cm

b i

h (mm)	r (mm)	V (mm^3)
6.8	4.9	**510**
34.8	21.3	**49600**
761	86.3	**17800000**
2.45	11.4	998.8

b ii

h (cm)	r (cm)	V (cm^3)
1.69	19.6	2041
1.49	24.6	2840
11.3	**4.88**	846.1
17.44	**3.771**	779.2

12 a i $r = \sqrt{\dfrac{833 \times 3}{14.8} \div \pi} \approx 7.33$ cm

b i

h (cm)	r (cm)	V (cm^3)
16.3	14.7	**3690**
28	13	**5000**
81.31	41.06	**143600**
15.2	23.8	9014

b ii

h (mm)	r (mm)	V (mm^3)
7.976	108.4	98143
61.4	**11.5**	8439
71.4	**102**	780639
22	**5.8**	777.8

13 a $1.67
   b $33
   c $518
   d $9.78

e $ .23
f $6.13

14 b i 0.618 = 61.8%
   b ii 0.095 = 9.5%
   b iii 0.891 = 89.1%
   b iv 0.0384 = 3.84%
   b v 0.0513 = 5.13%
   b vi 0.0780 = 7.80%
   b vii 0.63 = 63%
   b viii 0.62 = 62%

15 a By Method B: $319 ÷ 1.35 = about $236
   b i

CP ($)	Markup	SP ($)
914	31%	**1197**
741	28%	**948**
13406	81%	24265
29036	42%	41231

b ii

CP ($)	Markup	SP ($)
32	70%	55
729	21%	882
2811	−28%	**2024**
419	**70%**	713

16 a Method B: $48 × 0.70 = 33.6 or about $34
   b i

UP ($)	Discount	DP ($)
804	41%	**474**
9141	7%	**8501**
487	19%	**394**
4177	26%	3091

b ii

UP ($)	Discount	DP ($)
997	21%	788
20404	47%	10814
91	4%	**87**
814	14%	**700**

17 a Price = $298.50 × 1.083 ≈ $313.53
   b Price = $298.50 × 1.083 × 1.176 ≈ $368.71
   c $289.50 × 1.259 ≈ $364.48 ≠ $368.71 from **b**.

18 a $\dfrac{2A}{h} = b$, so 120 ÷ 10 = 12
   b i A (mm^2): 2 800, 3 000, 4 400, 7 000
   b ii

b (cm)	h (cm)	A (cm^2)
16	**10**	80
10	20	100
40	**10**	200
100	200	10000

19 a $y = 10$ cm, $P = 2 \times 10 + 2 \times 6 = 32$ cm

b i

x (cm)	y (cm)	P (cm)	A (cm^2)
6	8	**28**	**48**
10	14	**48**	**140**
8	12	**40**	**96**
10	8	**36**	80
20	8	**56**	160

b ii

x (cm)	y (cm)	P (cm)	A (cm^2)
4	5	**18**	**20**
9	9	**36**	**81**
6	**7**	26	**42**
7	10	34	**70**
6 or 5	**5 or 6**	22	30

20 a $T = (2 \times 13.8 \times 14.9) + (2 \times 14.9 \times 20.8) +$ $(2 \times 13 \times 20.8) \approx 1610$ cm^2 (3 sig figs)

b

$2xy$ (cm^2)	$2yz$ (cm^2)	$2xz$ (cm^2)
747.408	999.252	905.28
74283.48	35303.04	31415.04
1583344	447.6136	402.7568
100224	47865.6	28918.8
4.684598	12.34368	6.29568
1.696482	1.696482	1.696482

T (cm^2)	V (cm^3)
2650	9190
141000	3210000
1010	1890
177000	4160000
23.32	6.746
5.09	0.781

c 21.2 cm

d $x = y = z$. So $T = 2x^2 + 2x^2 + 2x^2 = 6x^2$

21 a i 2 units^2

a ii 3 units^2

a iii 3 units^2

a iv 3 units^2

b 14 units^2

c F = 5 units^2; G = 3 units^2; H = 3 units^2; I = 3 units^2; so E = 14 units^2

22 a If there are a runs in each inning and altogether there x innings, then there are ax runs scored. So $n = ax$.

b i 32 runs

b ii 20 runs

c

First Season		
Runs	Innings Completed	Average
2	13	0.15
10	26	0.38
8	41	0.20
5	12	**0.42**

Second Season			Average Over Two Seasons
Runs	Innings Completed	Average	
11	18	0.61	**0.42**
3	8	0.38	**0.38**
13	**18**	0.72	**0.36**
8	**15**	0.53	**0.48**

23 a Average speed $= \dfrac{12 - 7}{3 - 2} = 5$ ft/s

b Average speed $= \dfrac{14 - 12}{4 - 3} = 2$ ft/s

c Average speed $= \dfrac{15 - 3}{5 - 1} = 3$ ft/s

d Average speed (ft/s): 3, $3\frac{2}{3}$, $3\frac{1}{2}$, $2\frac{2}{3}$, $1\frac{1}{2}$, 1

24 a $c^2 = (11.6)^2 - (8.6)^2 = 60.6$, so $c \approx 7.8$

b i

b (m)	c (m)	a (m)
14.9	12.6	**19.5**
50.3	60.7	**78.8**
1.7	3.8	**4.2**
4.2	**4.1**	5.9
5.7	3.9	6.9

b ii

b (cm)	c (cm)	a (cm)
261.8	268.7	**375.2**
293.6	274.4	401.9
414.2	407.9	581.3
281.8	384.7	**476.9**
impossible	46.9	46.0

25

BC (mm)	AB (mm)	AC (mm)	α
35	50	36	44°
25	70	**65**	**21°**
35	65	**55**	**33°**
41	49	**27**	**57°**
53	68	**43**	**51°**

26 a i Bearing: 000°, 045°, 090°, 135°

a ii Compass point: S, SW, W, NW

b i

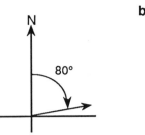

b ii

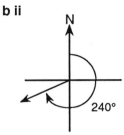

b iii

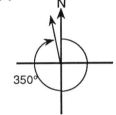

b iv

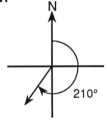

b v

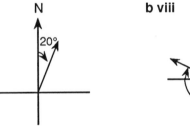

b vi

b vii

b viii

27 a $(-3 \times -2) - (-5 \times 2) = 6 - (-10) = 16$
b i -6
b ii -2
b iii 2
b iv -10
b v 0
b vi -8
b vii 10
b viii 2

28 a 2^4
 b 2^3
 c 2^2
 d 2^1
 e 2^0
 f 64
 g 256
 h 81
 i 1000
 j 125
 k 64
 l 1

29 a $2x(3x-4) = 2x \times 3x - 2x \times 4 = 6x^2 - 8x$
 b i $12x^2 + 9x$
 b ii $2x - 4x^2$
 b iii $3x - 4x^2$
 b iv $3y^2 + y$
 b v $4y^2 + 3y$
 b vi $14y - 6y^2$
 b vii $y^2 + 7y$
 b viii $3f^2 - f$

30 a $z = xy = x \times 2x^2 = 2x^3$
 b i $z = 3x^3$
 b ii $z = x^3$
 b iii $z = 4x^4$
 b iv $z = 32r^4$
 b v $z = 4x^3$
 b vi $z = 2x^3$

31 a

x	C ($)	Pattern
1	19	$(1 \times 15) + 4$
2	34	$(2 \times 15) + 4$
3	49	$(3 \times 15) + 4$
4	64	$(4 \times 15) + 4$
5	79	$(5 \times 15) + 4$

b $C = 15x + 4$
c i $C = 4x + 1$
c ii $C = 3x + 4$
c iii $C = 5x + 4$

32 b $\$12.50 \times 1.727\,272\,7 = \$21.59$
 c

Scale Factor (unrounded)	Cost of Length B ($)
1.7272727	21.59
1.5714286	57.20
6.2352941	556.19
1.16	132.82
0.6	22.05
0.4666667	42.58

33 a (1,3), (2,5), (3,7), (6,13)
 b (5,3), (2,2), (−4,0), (11,5)
 c (3,5), (2,3), (4,7), (5,9)
 d (1,6), (4,3), (3,4), (7,0)
 e (0,6), (3,4), (0,6), (6,2)
 f (0,15), (3,10), (6,5), (0,15)

34
 a

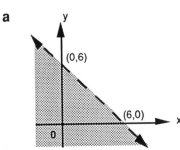

b

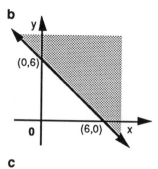

c

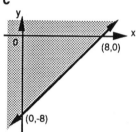

d

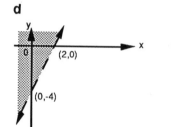

e

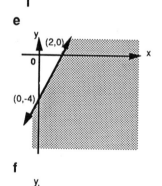

f

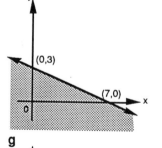

g

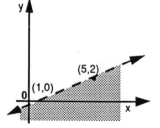

h

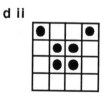

i

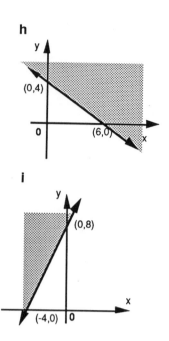

35 There are many possible answers. For example:

a i 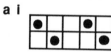 **a ii**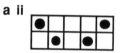

b i **b ii**

c i **c ii**

d i Not possible, as rotations always produce line symmetry, also.

d ii

ANSWER KEY

INVESTIGATIONS

INVESTIGATIONS

Answer Key

CHAPTER 1   GEOMETRY

Investigation One – Symmetry

1   **a** Flooring and roofing costs depend on the area of the house, whereas wall costs depend on the perimeter.

c i

x	y	P
1	64	130
2	32	68
4	16	40
8	8	32
16	4	40
32	2	68
64	1	130

c ii Costs will be minimized by having the smallest perimeter which, from the table, is a square where $x = y = 8$. So $P = 32$.

d i

x	y	A
0	16	0
2	14	28
4	12	48
6	10	60
8	8	64
10	6	60
12	4	48
14	2	28
16	0	0

d ii The 8×8 rectangle (square)

e Both are squares.

f i 9×9 square

f ii 36 m

g i Square

g ii 100 m^2

2   **a** 48 unit^2

b ii 50 unit^2

c i 50 unit^2

c ii A square is the most symmetrical rectangle.

d i *Hint:* The most symmetrical triangle is isosceles in this case.

d ii 25 unit^2

d iii *Hint:* Notice the isosceles triangle is half of the square in **b i.**

3   **a** $3^2 + h^2 = 12^2$, so $h^2 = 144 - 9 = 135$, and $h = \sqrt{135}$

b $A = 1/2bh = 3 \times h) \approx 3 \times 11.62 = 34.86$ units^2

c Because the most symmetrical triangle is equilateral.

d i

x	y	h	Area
14	1	$\sqrt{195}$	13.96
13	2	$\sqrt{165}$	25.69
12	3	$\sqrt{135}$	34.86
11	4	$\sqrt{105}$	40.99
10	5	$\sqrt{75}$	43.30
9	6	$\sqrt{45}$	40.25
8	7	$\sqrt{15}$	27.11
7	8	impossible	–

d ii Yes

e When $x \leq 7.5$ or $x \geq 15$, the triangle does not exist.

f Equilateral

4   ΔB has the maximum area because it has the most symmetry.

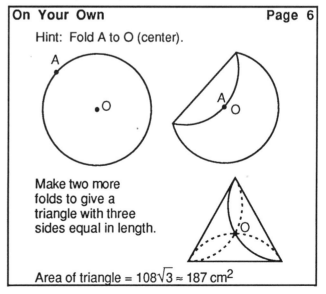

On Your Own   **Page 6**

Hint: Fold A to O (center).

Make two more folds to give a triangle with three sides equal in length.

Area of triangle = $108\sqrt{3} \approx 187$ cm^2

5 a A square is more symmetrical than an equilateral triangle.
b The square has an area greater than that of the triangle by 1900 m².
c Yes, because a regular pentagon has more symmetry than a square.
d i △ABC is equilateral; area = 1 558.845 7 m².
d ii 9400 m²
e The regular hexagon, because it is the most symmetrical.

6 a The circle, because it is more symmetrical than the square.
b i 19.735 213 cm
b ii About 1 220 cm²

7 a The circle, because it is more symmetrical.
b $\sqrt{121} = 11$ and $11 \times 4 = 44$
c i $r \approx 6.206\ 085\ 3$ m
c ii About 39.0 m

8 a Shape A has the minimum perimeter because it is the most symmetrical shape.
b Shape B has the maximum perimeter because it is the least symmetrical shape.

9 a Yes
b Yes
c i 1 600 m²
c ii 1 750 m²
d No, the use of the existing fence makes her principle invalid in this case.
e length = 60 m; width = 30 m; area = 1 800 m²

On Your Own   **Page 9**
The shape with maximum area is a circle because it is the plane figure with the most symmetry.

---

10 a The hexagon, using the principle of greatest symmetry.
b No shape has more symmetry than a circle.
c Design B
d *Hint:* Try half a circle.

11 a A cube
b 10 cm × 10 cm × 10 cm
c i

2xy	2xz	2yz	T (cm²)
2	2000	2000	4002
4	1000	2000	3004
10	400	2000	2410
20	200	2000	2220
8	500	500	1008

As the cuboid → cube, $T \to 600$ cm², which is the minimum surface area.
c ii Yes
d i A cube 10 cm on a side

On Your Own   **Page 10**
1 If the carton was closed, the optimal shape would be a cube. The optimal shape for an open carton such as this will be half of an 8000 cm³ cube. (Two halves can be fitted together to make the optimal cube.)
2 Base = 20 cm × 20 cm; height = 10 cm.

---

12 a The ball
b Possibly; a spherical egg would have less shell and therefore might be more efficient to produce.
c A spherical egg would be more difficult for the hen to lay.
13 Design B, because it has the most symmetrical cross section, and therefore the least surface area to be subjected to the water pressure.

Investigation Two − Biology

1 a i

Number of Faces Exposed to Heat			
Block A	Block B	Block C	Total
5	4	5	1 4
6	6	6	1 8

a ii The broken-apart cubes will melt more quickly because more surface area is exposed to the air than is the case with the single block.
b i A cube has 6 faces, so 27 cubes will have 162 faces exposed.
b ii On a single side of the large block, 9 small cube faces are exposed, and $6 \times 9 = 54$.
b iii Yes, because less surface is exposed.
c Stack the eight blocks to make a large cube, $2 \times 2 \times 2$; this cube is the most symmetrical shape possible using the 8 blocks.
2 A sphere, because it has the most symmetry and the smallest surface area.
3 a Crushed ice, because it has more surface area exposed.
b A block of ice; the crushed ice is likely to melt before the weekend is over because it has more surface area exposed.
4 Kool Kustomers will be able to supply more water; their ice will last longer because less of it is exposed (their iceberg has the smaller surface area).
5 Make the 50 smaller cubes, because these cubes will have in total much more surface area exposed than the single large cube, so the heat can be transferred more quickly.
6 a The son
b For similar-shaped objects, the smallest heats up or cools down faster than the largest.
c Yes, because this reduces his surface area.

7 The eight 200 g packs would be better because more surface area is exposed, so that the heat energy transfer (loss) from the food and drink to the freezer packs is more rapid.

8 a *Hint:* Find out about the strong cooling effect of evaporation.
   b Both father and daughter need to lose excess heat on a hot day. Because his daughter is small, she does this relatively easily and does not need to sweat as much to aid her cooling.

9 They should huddle together to reduce their external surface area.

10 The soft drink will be cooler in the larger bottle as it heats up more slowly than a similar small bottle.

11 a 48 000 heat units for 8 bricks
   b

	Surface Area (cm^2)	Heat Loss in One Minute (Units)
Small cube	600	600
Large cube	2400	2400

   c i 600 = 10% of 6000
   c ii 2400 = 5% of 48 000
   d Large objects have proportionally less surface area than similarly-shaped small objects.
   e Because they have more surface area relative to their volume, children will lose body heat more quickly when exposed to extreme cold.
   f Assuming that the whale and the dolphin are at the same body temperature, the whale cannot as easily get rid of its excess heat, because it has less surface area relative to volume than the dolphin.

12 a Mark would eat 25 kg of food.
   b Very much less than 25 kg.
   c The mouse, relatively speaking, loses much more heat than a human, and so must eat a relatively large amount to generate enough heat.
   d i Curve c. We can eliminate curve a as it shows P decreasing, then increasing. Because curve b is a straight line, it implies that for a heavy animal, such as an elephant, P can become a negative value; this is absurd. Curve d shows that P increases as W increases. This cannot be true. The error in reasoning is that the *percentage* eaten has been confused with the *amount* eaten. Only curve c makes sense.
   d ii A mammal that small would lose heat faster than it could eat to supply the necessary energy.

13 a All animals need a certain blood temperature to become active. Lizards are cold-blooded, and so take on the temperature of their environment. If this is below the critical temperature for movement, the lizard will not move normally until the environment becomes warmer.
   b The small one
   c The large one

14 a More surface area where reactions can take place would be exposed by crushing the lump.
   b Even in a small lump of crushed sugar, there are many molecules inside the lump that the yeast cannot reach to promote the reaction. Stirring will separate the molecules so the yeast can react with every molecule, and the reaction will proceed much more quickly.

15 Piece B. Piece A is closer in shape to a sphere than piece B. As A and B have equal weight (and volume), B has the greater surface area and will dissolve more quickly in the mouth.

On Your Own   Page 18
1 When hair gets dirty, it is covered with a build-up of oil. Shampoo breaks down the oil on the hair into very small droplets that can be easily washed away.
2 Soaps work by lowering the surface tension of the water. Water forms a thin, almost elastic skin over a dirty or greasy surface; this property is called surface tension. Soapy water has much less surface tension, and enables the water to better wash away the dirt or grease. The dirt is absorbed by the suds and held in the soapy water until it is rinsed away. Agitation or rubbing helps loosen the dirt so it can be collected in the soapsuds.

---

3 Bile emulsifies fats (breaks the fat down) to a size that can be taken into the bloodstream through the wall of the stomach.

Investigation
Three – Container Design

1 420 cm^3
2 a Volume of a cylinder = $\pi r^2 h$
   b The area of each end is πr^2 and the area of the curved surface is $2\pi rh$.
   c i $r = 3.076\ 367\ 2$
   c ii 276 cm^2
   d i

h (cm)	r (cm)	S (cm^2)
15.0	2.6582851	295
12.5	2.9120054	282
10.0	3.2557209	271
7.5	3.7593828	270
5.0	4.6042847	278

   d ii

h (cm)	r (cm)	S (cm^2)
4.5	4.8533423	290
3.6	5.4262017	310
2.8	6.1527344	350
2.4	6.6457127	380
1.2	9.398457	630

---

e i When $h = d = 2r$, the cylinder has the most symmetry.

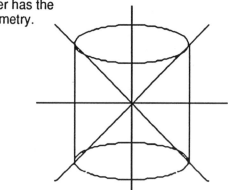

e ii Minimum S occurs near $h = 7.5$ cm, but further investigation on either side of this height is necessary to confirm that the minimum surface area for a cylinder with fixed volume occurs when $h = 2r$.

3 b Yes

4 a $V = \pi r^2 h$. But $h = 2r$, so $V = \pi r^2 \times 2r = 2\pi r^3$

b

V	r (cm)	S (cm²)
1000 ml	5.4192607	554
2000 ml	6.8278406	879
3.0 L	7.8159264	1151
4.0 L	8.6025401	1395
5.8 L	9.7367953	1787

On Your Own   **Page 20**

The optimal shape for a can occurs when the height equals the diameter ($h = 2r$). This design requires the least amount of metal for a given volume. Most food cans are designed with the height longer than the diameter, however, making them easier to hold.

---

5 a The minimum surface area for a closed cylinder occurs when $h = 2r$. Imagine the open cylinder to be half of the closed cylinder. The open cylinder will have minimum surface area when its height is one-half that of the closed cylinder, that is, when $h = r$.
b i 5.572 667 5 cm
b ii 1530 cm² (2 sig. figs.)
c The area of the bottom $= \pi r^2$, and the area of the curved part $= 2\pi rh$.
d i

h (cm)	r (cm)	S (cm²)
18.2	8.3641029	1176
14.8	9.2752196	1133
12.7	10.012746	1114
10.8	10.857834	1107
9.7	11.456955	1111

d ii

h (cm)	r (cm)	S (cm²)
8.6	12.167625	1123
7.9	12.695257	1136
6.3	14.216241	1198
4.8	16.28675	1325
2.6	22.129336	1900

e Yes

6 a $V = \pi r^2 \times h$ and $h = r$, so $V = \pi r^2 \times r = \pi r^3$

b

V	r (cm)	S (cm²)
5000 ml	11.675443	1285
6.0 L	12.407010	1451
6.7 L	12.871870	1562
5.0 L	11.675443	1285
5.8 L	12.267593	1418
500 ml	5.4192607	277

7 a i $r = 7.496\ 197\ 8$ cm
a ii 3420 cm³
b i 1410 cm³
b ii No
c Cylinder A

8 a 124 000 cm³
b i One might think that because the respective radii and heights have been interchanged, the volumes will be the same. This is not correct. From the results of problem **7**, the sensible prediction here is that the cone with the greater base area (greater radius) will have the greater volume.
b ii Volume of A = 12400 cm³; volume of B = 6320 cm³
c For a cone with radius r and height h,
$V = \frac{1}{3}\pi r^2 h$. When $y > x$, $\frac{1}{3}\pi y^2 x > \frac{1}{3}\pi x^2 y$. So Cone A has the greater volume.

On Your Own   **Page 23**

The surface area of the cone is $S = \pi rl$ and the volume is $V = \frac{1}{3}\pi r^2 h$ where r = radius of base, l = length from point to edge, and h = height from point to center of base. For a fixed volume of 56.8 L, find the minimum surface area by a systematic search. For example, if we allow that $\frac{1}{3}\pi \approx 1$, then $56.8 = r^2 h$ or $h = \dfrac{56.8}{r^2}$. For various lengths of r (in cm), we can calculate corresponding heights. Construct cones of each size and calculate the surface area by measuring l and using the formula $S = \pi rl$. The surface area can be calculated directly using the equivalent formula $S = \pi r\sqrt{h^2 + r^2}$.

Class Investigation   Page 23

a i Because the circumference of the circle wraps around the cone twice.

a ii Because the cone has a circumference one-half that of the original circle.

b Because all three sides equal the radius.

c i The size of angle m is 60°, which is the angle of filter fiunnels used in everyday situations.

c ii The angle 60° allows the maximum amount of fluid to be contained in a funnel.

CHAPTER ONE – CHECK-UP

1 **a** *Number of sides:* 3, 4, 5, 6
Length of sides (m): 100, 75, 60, 50
b i The circle is the most symmetrical shape and thus yields the maximum area.
b ii Radius = 47.75 m; area = 7162 m^2

2 C, B, A

3 **a** The cylinder has more symmetry than a cuboid and so, for equal volumes, has less surface area.
b i About 6.8 cm
b ii About 13.7 cm
c No. A cylinder with height equal to diameter (as in **b**) has more symmetry than the cube.
d Such containers can be packed into shipping cartons with no gaps; this is more efficient than cylinders, which leave gaps.
e The current container, because it has greater surface area.

4 **a** 14.7 cm
b 14.7 cm
c i $r \approx 11.7$ cm, $h \approx 23.4$ cm
c ii 2 140 cm^2 (*Hint:* Remember to use unrounded r and h.)
c iii For the minimal design, $S \approx 2039$ cm^2.
Saving = 2140 − 2039 = 101 cm^2.
Percentage saving = 101 ÷ 2039 ≈ 5%.

5 Spherical shapes have the most symmetry of any containers and so are the best design for minimum surface area. Teapots are often given a roughly spherical design *not* to minimize costs, but to minimize heat loss via the minimum surface area.

CHAPTER 2   PATTERNS

Investigation One – Patterns

1 **a i** 4 grandparents
    a ii 8 great-grandparents

b i

Generations Back	Number in Generation	Pattern
0	1	2^0
1	2	2^1
2	4	2^2
3	8	2^3
4	16	2^4
5	32	2^5
6	64	2^6
n		2^n

b ii About 20 ($2^{20} = 1\ 048\ 576$)
c Tom had 10 000 000 ancestors about 23 or 24 generations back, which is about 575 to 600 years ago.
e As anyone's family tree is drawn further backwards, it becomes virtually certain that some individual ancestors appear as multiple entries in the tree; therefore the number of ancestors will be lower than predicted using the formula in **b i.**

2 **b i** The number in a generation is found by adding the numbers in the previous two generations, producing the sequence 1, 1, 2, 3, 5, 8, 13, 21, . . .
b ii 233 bees

On Your Own   Page 30

1

Beginning of Month	Total Pairs of Rabbits
1	1
2	1
3	2
4	3
5	5
6	8
7	13
8	21
9	34
10	55
11	89
12	144
13	233

2 This diagram shows 13 keys that represent one octave of the chromatic scale on a piano keyboard.

There are 8 white keys in this octave, the notes of a major scale. The 5 black keys are the notes of the old pentatonic scale. (13 = 5 + 8)

3 b

four disks

1	2	3
abcd		
abc	d	
ab	d	c
ab		cd
a	b	cd
ad	b	c
ad	bc	
a	bcd	
	bcd	a
	bc	ad
c	b	ad
cd	b	a
cd		ab
c		ab
	d	abc
	d	abcd

c

Number of Disks	Minimum Number of Moves	Pattern
1	1	$2^1 - 1$
2	3	$2^2 - 1$
3	7	$2^3 - 1$
4	**15**	$2^4 - 1$
5	**31**	$2^5 - 1$
6	**63**	$2^6 - 1$
⋮	⋮	⋮
n		$2^n - 1$

d i About 18 000 000 000 000 000 000 moves.
d ii To move 64 disks would take about 580 billion years, so there is no need to worry even if the legend is true.
e i Yes
e ii The top 6 disks will take 63 moves to transfer to tower 2. The seventh disk can move from tower 1 to tower 3 in a single move and the six disks in tower 2 require a further 63 moves to transfer to tower 3. Altogether, $63 + 1 + 63 = 127$ moves are required.

4 a Number of regions: 1, 2, 4, 8, 16
b i A sensible prediction is 32.
b ii In fact, the answer is 31.
c i Number of regions: 1, 2, 4, 8, 16, 31, **57, 99**
First difference: 1, 2, 4, 8, 15, **26, 42**
Second difference: 1, 2, 4, 7, **11, 16**
Third difference: 1, 2, 3, **4, 5**
c ii No. *Any* pattern might break down eventually.

5 a

Trees on Boundary (*b*)

3	4	5	6	7
$\frac{1}{2}$	1	$1\frac{1}{2}$	2	$2\frac{1}{2}$
$1\frac{1}{2}$	2	$2\frac{1}{2}$	3	$3\frac{1}{2}$
$2\frac{1}{2}$	3	$3\frac{1}{2}$	4	$4\frac{1}{2}$
$3\frac{1}{2}$	4	$4\frac{1}{2}$	5	$5\frac{1}{2}$
$4\frac{1}{2}$	5	$5\frac{1}{2}$	6	$6\frac{1}{2}$
$5\frac{1}{2}$	6	$6\frac{1}{2}$	7	$7\frac{1}{2}$

b i Notice the area increases by $\frac{1}{2}$ going across a row and by 1 going down a column.
b ii These combinations of *b* and *i* are impossible.
c i

b	A	Pattern
3	$\frac{1}{2}$	$\frac{1}{2} \times 3 - 1$
4	1	$\frac{1}{2} \times 4 - 1$
5	$1\frac{1}{2}$	$\frac{1}{2} \times 5 - 1$
6	2	$\frac{1}{2} \times 6 - 1$
7	$2\frac{1}{2}$	$\frac{1}{2} \times 7 - 1$
⋮	⋮	⋮
b		$\frac{1}{2}b - 1$

c ii $A = \frac{1}{2}b - 1$
d i $A = \frac{1}{2}b$
d ii $A = \frac{1}{2}b + 1$
d iii $A = \frac{1}{2}b + 2$
d iv $A = \frac{1}{2}b + 3$

e i

i	Formula for A	Pattern
0	$A = \frac{1}{2}b - 1$	$A = \frac{1}{2}b + 0 - 1$
1	$A = \frac{1}{2}b$	$A = \frac{1}{2}b + 1 - 1$
2	$A = \frac{1}{2}b + 1$	$A = \frac{1}{2}b + 2 - 1$
3	$A = \frac{1}{2}b + 2$	$A = \frac{1}{2}b + 3 - 1$
4	$A = \frac{1}{2}b + 3$	$A = \frac{1}{2}b + 4 - 1$
5	$A = \frac{1}{2}b + 4$	$A = \frac{1}{2}b + 5 - 1$
$\vdots$	$\vdots$	$\vdots$
i		$A = \frac{1}{2}b + i - 1$

e ii $b = 24$, $i = 17$ gives area of the orchard as 28 squares. Each square is 25 m^2, so area of the orchard is 700 m^2 = 0.07 hectare.

On Your Own   **Page 35**

For n ponds, the formula is $A = \frac{1}{2}b + i + n - 1$.

---

6 **a** The sums of two consecutive whole numbers are $1 + 2 = 3$, $2 + 3 = 5$, $3 + 4 = 7$, $4 + 5 = 9$, and so on. The sums of three consecutive whole numbers are $1 + 2 + 3 = 6$, $2 + 3 + 4 = 9$, and so on. For four consecutive whole numbers, the sums are $1 + 2 + 3 + 4 = 10$ and so on. By a systematic search, we find that none of these totals is 8.
b i Yes, 14 and 15
b ii Every odd number from 3 onward.
c i 6, 9, 12 . . .
c ii 10, 14, 18 . . .
c iii 15, 20, 25 . . .
c iv 21, 27, 33 . . .
d The only impossible totals are of the form 2^n.
e Only **i** and **iii** are the sum of consecutive whole numbers.
7 **c** Only the prime numbers are impossible.
d Only **ii, iii,** and **iv** can be made; 17 and 53 are prime.
8 **c ii** 1, 4, 9, 16, 25
d All are perfect squares.

---

f i

Ticket Number	Flip on	Number of Flips	Winner/Loser
1	1	1	winner
2	1, 2	2	loser
3	1, 3	2	**loser**
4	1, 2, 4	3	**winner**
5	1, 5	2	**loser**
6	1, 2, 3, 6	4	**loser**
7	1, 7	2	**loser**
8	1, 2, 4, 8	4	**loser**
9	1, 3, 9	3	**winner**
10	1, 2, 5, 10	4	**loser**

ii An odd number of flips results in a win, because square numbers have a repeated factor (1×1, 2×2, 3×3, and so on). This results in an odd number of factors.

Investigation
Two – Game Strategies

1 **a** The opponent takes *all* the remaining pile and wins.
b

Pile A	Pile B	First Move by Paul	Winner
1	1	1 from A	Kathy
1	1	1 from B	Kathy
2	1	1 from B	Kathy
2	1	2 from A	**Kathy**
2	1	1 from A	**Paul**
2	2	2 from A	Kathy
2	2	2 from B	**Kathy**

c ii Paul takes 5 from A leaving A = 2, B = 2. If Kathy takes 2 from either pile, Paul wins and if Kathy takes 1, Paul matches Kathy's move, ensuring each pile is left with 1. Kathy must take one of the remaining counters, thus ensuring a win for Paul.
d Kathy
e You will win by making sure that both piles have the same number of counters *after* each of your turns.
g If $A \neq B$, Paul takes enough from one pile to make A = B. Then whatever Kathy does to one pile, Paul does the same to the other. Paul will eventually win. If A = B to start, Kathy uses the same strategy as Paul and so wins.

On Your Own   **Page 39**

One approach is to remove all the counters in one pile when the other two piles have an equal number of counters. Never do this to leave unequal piles, allowing your opponent to then create two equal piles of counters.

---

2 b If you start, knock out the middle pin (or pins, if there are an even number of pins). Thereafter each of your moves should be the mirror image of your opponent's move.

c The winning player makes sure that the pins left standing after his/her move are symmetrical about the center.

3 c The first player puts down one or two counters in the center (whichever leaves a symmetrical shape). Then the first player can win by leaving a symmetrical shape after each turn.

d i Play second to win.

d ii First player puts counters in two squares in center and can always win by preserving symmetry.

d iii Play second to win.

d iv Same as for *d ii.*

d v Play second to win. (Second player can always win on an even × even grid.)

e i First player can win by putting a counter in the center square and preserving point symmetry thereafter.

e ii Put counters in two center squares and maintain point symmetry.

e iii Same as for *e i.*

e iv Same as for *e ii.*

f i

Winners for Various Grid Sizes

	1	2	3	4	5	6
1	1st	1st	1st	1st	1st	1st
2	1st	2nd	1st	2nd	1st	2nd
3	1st	1st	1st	1st	1st	1st
4	1st	2nd	1st	2nd	1st	2nd
5	1st	1st	1st	1st	1st	1st
6	1st	2nd	1st	2nd	1st	2nd

f ii The first player puts 1 or 2 counters in the center (which is not possible for an even × even grid) and then copies each of the opposing player's moves in a way that preserves point symmetry.

On Your Own   **Page 41**
The first player who moves to the space immediately in front of the opponent's counter will lose, provided the second player plays sensibly. A winning strategy is to always leave at least one space between the two counters in a column and so force your opponent to move to the space next to your counter.

4 a i Anthony wins because Simone can only take away 1, which is not allowed by the rules.

b i You win.

b ii Opponent wins.

c i Subtract 1 to ensure a win.

c ii Subtract 2 to ensure a loss.

d i

Number Left for Simone	Factor Subtracted	Number Left for Anthony	Winner
2	1	1	Simone
3	1	2	**Anthony**
4	2	2	**Anthony**
4	1	3	**Simone**
5	1	4	**Anthony**
6	3	3	**Simone**
6	2	4	**Anthony**
6	1	5	**Simone**
8	4	4	**Anthony**
8	2	6	**Anthony**
8	1	7	**Simone**
9	3	6	**Anthony**
9	1	8	**Anthony**
10	5	5	**Simone**
10	2	8	**Anthony**
10	1	9	**Simone**

Simone makes sure the number left for Anthony is *always* odd.

d ii Subtract 1 or 3. This ensures that Anthony is left with an odd number and therefore loses.

e *Hint:* Explain why you must not leave 4 after your move and how you can prevent this.

On Your Own   **Page 42**
The player who goes second can always win by maintaining symmetry. That is, whatever counter(s) the first player removes, the second player moves corresponding counter(s) to leave a symmetrical pattern. To find the strategy, it is helpful to first try simpler polygons (triangle, square).

5 a

Beginning Total	First Number Subtracted by A	Eventual Winner Must Be . . .
1	1	B
2	1	A
2	2	B
3	1	B
3	2	A
4	1	B
4	**2**	B
5	1	B

b 1, 4, 7, 10 . . . or $3n - 2$

c i Player A

c ii Player B

c iii Player A

c iv Player B

c v Player A

6 In order to win, the current total *after* your move must be as follows:
a 1, 5, 9, 13 . . . or $4n-3$
b i 1, 6, 11, 16 . . . or $5n-4$
b ii 1, 7, 13, 19 . . . or $6n-5$
b iii 1, 8, 15, 23 . . . or $7n-6$
c 1, $n+2$, $2n+3$, $3n+4$ . . .

7 Make sure the current total after your turn is 11, 22, 33, 44 . . .

8 **a i** Laura can select up to $2 \times 9 = 18$. There are only $26-9 = 17$ left, so Laura subtracts 17 and wins.

a ii Double 8 or less is 16 or less. $26-8 = 18$. So Laura cannot subtract enough to win in her next move.

a iii If she takes one-third or more, the rules allow her opponent to take the remaining two-thirds (or fewer) in the next move.

b i Elizabeth can take either 1 or 2 (one-third or more) and so loses.

b ii Laura can only take away 1, leaving Elizabeth with 4, who in turn takes away 1 leaving Laura with 3. By the reasoning in problem **b i**, Elizabeth must win.

c i Laura notices that, because Elizabeth can only take away less than one-third of the total left to her, she cannot leave a total that is the next Fibonacci number down in the sequence.

c ii Yes, provided she can find a way to force the non-Fibonacci total left by Elizabeth back to a Fibonacci number.

d i Laura can take 1 or 2, leaving Elizabeth to take 2 or 1 respectively, and so forcing the total to 13 in either case.

d ii Yes. When playing from a non-Fibonacci number, a player can force a win by subtracting the smallest Fibonacci number appearing in the representation. This succeeds because with any two nonconsecutive Fibonacci numbers, the smaller one is always less than one-half the larger.

CHAPTER TWO – CHECK-UP

1 **a** The pattern in the total number of amounts is $2^n - 1$. There are altogether $2^n - 1$ subsets (excluding the empty set) in a set with n members.
b $2^{12} - 1 = 4095$ amounts

2 **a** There is only one move to win.

b

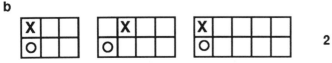

c The first player should aim for either square marked ●.

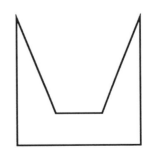

d The winner is the one who always moves to a square that is an odd number of rows and columns from the Finish.
e Same as for **d** above.
f i

Winners for Various Grid Sizes

		Grid Width				
	2	**3**	**4**	**5**	**6**	**7**
2	2nd	2nd	2nd	2nd	2nd	2nd
3	2nd	1st	2nd	1st	2nd	1st
4	2nd	2nd	2nd	2nd	2nd	2nd
5	2nd	1st	2nd	1st	2nd	1st
6	2nd	2nd	2nd	2nd	2nd	2nd
7	2nd	1st	2nd	1st	2nd	1st

f ii You can force a win if, after you take a turn, you are on a square that is an odd number of rows and columns from the Finish.

CHAPTER 3
OPERATIONS RESEARCH

Investigation
One – Guarding the Gallery

1 **a i** At point B or point D. Notice that point B is better because the camera has to turn through only an acute angle ($< 90°$) at B, but through a reflex angle ($> 180°$) at D.
a ii No
b i 1
b ii At point E
b iii No
c One possible design would be:

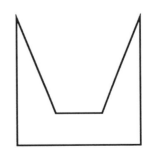

2 **a** No
b i At point B
b ii At any corner of $\triangle CDE$

c i {B,E}, {B,C}, {B,D}
c ii {E,F}, {E,A}, {E,B}
c iii {B,E}, {B,C}, {F,E}, {F,C}
c iv {C,F}, {C,A}, {E,F}, {E,A}
c v {B,E}, {B,C}, {F,E}, {F,C}, {A,E}, {A,C}
c vi {B,C}, {B,D}
c vii {B,E}, {B,D}. Cameras located at A and C are best because at those positions, the camera has to turn through the smallest angles (both acute).
d i DF added gives cameras at {C,E}, {C,F}, {C,D}, {A,E}, {A,D}, and {A,F}; AC added gives cameras at {D,A}, {D,B}, {D,C}, {F,B} and {F,C}. {A,E} is best because ∠E is less than ∠B.
d ii One camera at C is sufficient.
d iii One camera at F is sufficient.
d iv One camera at F will guard the heptagon ACDEFGH. So {F,A}, {F,B}, and {F,C} are possible locations with {F,B} being the best because ∠B is the smallest of ∠A, ∠B, or ∠C.

e i

Gallery Shape	Imaginary Wall Installed to Form
hexagon	pentagon + triangle
heptagon	pentagon + **quadrilateral**
octagon	pentagon + **pentagon**

e ii Since an octagon can be divided into two pentagons, and a pentagon requires only one camera, any octagon requires at most two cameras.

f

No. of Sides of Gallery	Number of Pentagons Possible	Shape Remaining	Number of Cameras for Worst Case
3	0	triangle	1
4	0	quadrilateral	1
5	1	—	1
6	1	triangle	2
7	1	**quadrilateral**	2
8	2	—	2
9	2	**triangle**	3
10	2	**quadrilateral**	3
11	3	—	3
12	3	**triangle**	4

3 **a** *c*: 1, 1, 1, 2, 2, 2, 3, 3, 3, 4
b i 6 cameras
b ii 16 cameras
b iii 34 cameras
c The number of cameras required in the worst case is $n \div 3$, ignoring any remainder.

d i

d ii

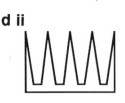

d iii

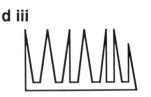

Investigation Two – Forecasting

1 **a-b**

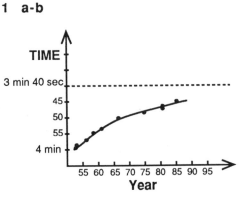

c The rate of improvement is decreasing. If the improvement follows the curve, the record could be 3 min 40 s by the year 2020. This could be absolutely wrong, however, because humans may never be able to run at this speed for a mile.
c ii Present trends indicate that this will never be reached.

2 **a-b**

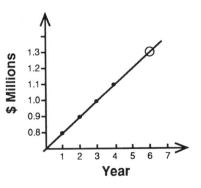

c If sales continue to increase at about $100 000 per year, the publishing house will have to move after year 6.

3 a

b i About $13.87
b ii About $14.03
b iii About $14.44
c No accurate assumptions can be made beyond week 8 because, for example, there may be a slump or crash in prices in week 9 or later.
4 a Sales of sunglasses are greater in summer because there is more need for them then.
b-c

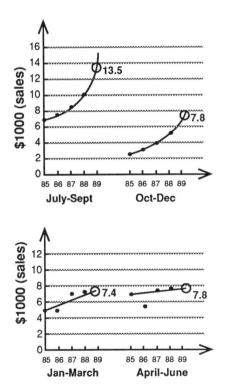

d No great certainty should be attached to the predictions because there are so many variables in the marketplace; that is, production costs may soar, leading to high prices that depress sales; competing companies may get a larger share of the market for any number of reasons; an unusually cold summer may keep people indoors and not buying sunglasses, and so forth.

Investigation Three – Traveling Sales Rep Problem

1 a

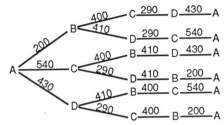

Route	Distance (km)
ABCDA	1320
ABDCA	**1440**
ACBDA	1780
ACDBA	**1440**
ADBCA	1780
ADCBA	**1320**

b ABCDA, 1320 km
c i Yes
c ii Because each route found from the tree diagram occurs twice (once in each direction), the total number of routes in **a** must be divided by 2.
2 a HAGNH, or the reverse route HNGAH
b No
3 a WMXNDW, or the reverse route WDNXMW
b The same as **a,** except the starting point is M.
4 EDABCE or ECBADE
5 b CBAEDC or CDEABC
6 b The number of branches of the tree is too large to handle easily, so a method based on stretching rubber bands over nails or pegs is useful. Notice that this method may not give the optimal solution, but it will quickly lead to a good answer once the materials have been prepared.

7 a

Number of Towns	Number of Routes	Pattern
3	2	2!
4	6	3!
5	24	4!
6	**120**	**5 !**
7	720	6 !
8	**5040**	**7 !**
9	40320	8 !

For n towns there are $(n-1)!$ routes, or, if reverse routes are not counted as different, $(n-1)! \div 2$.

b i More than 1.2×10^{17}
b ii About 4 000 years
c No; in fact, problems involving large n are not simple to solve.

Investigation
Four – Mazes and Caving

3 *Hint:* When traversing the maze, regard the exit as a dead end.

5 **a** No, because the rule works only for connected mazes.
b None, because the left-hand-traversal rule will always allow them to return to the start. (They might not find John, however.)

6 No, because the place where Eric has collapsed is disconnected from the rest of the maze.

7 **b** The left-hand-traversal rule will work provided the maze is connected.

8 The extraordinary thing about the rules given here is that they work even when there is no map of the cave system.

9 Yes

Class Investigation	Page 63
No one should find a design for which the rules fail; these rules will always work.	

On Your Own	Page 63
1 Peter is correct.	
2 Any connected maze can be reduced to the following simple maze:	

CHAPTER THREE – CHECK-UP

1 This is one possible solution.

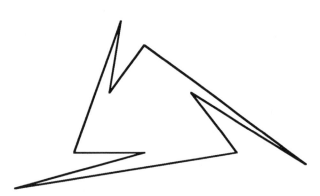

2 There are many possible solutions, provided the rules (Investigation Four, problem **8**) are followed.

3 **a** XACBX or reverse
b XABECDX or reverse

---

4 **a**

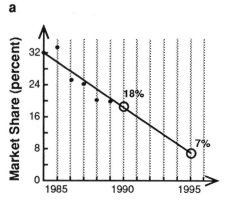

b i About 18%
b ii About 7%. While the 1990 prediction could be close, the 1995 prediction might be very wrong, as much can change in 5 years.

CHAPTER 4   PHOTOGRAPHY

Investigation
One – Shutter Times and f-Stops

1 a $\frac{1}{125}$ s

b Yes, because the exposure time has doubled.
c i Halving
c ii For convenience, shutter times greater than $\frac{1}{125}$ s are rounded.

d i

Exposure Time (s)	Light Intensity (units)
$\frac{1}{250}$	1
$\frac{1}{125}$	$\frac{1}{2}$
$\frac{1}{60}$	$\frac{1}{4}$
$\frac{1}{30}$	$\frac{1}{8}$
$\frac{1}{15}$	$\frac{1}{16}$

d ii

Exposure Time (s)	Light Intensity (units)
$\frac{1}{8}$	$\frac{1}{32}$
$\frac{1}{4}$	$\frac{1}{64}$
$\frac{1}{2}$	$\frac{1}{128}$
$\frac{1}{500}$	2
$\frac{1}{1000}$	4

2 **a** A shorter exposure time reduces the blurring.
b It is hard for people to keep their hands steady for longer than $\frac{1}{30}$ s, so when exposure times are any longer than that, hand wobble will likely cause a blurred photo.

3 **a** Doubling the aperture area doubles the amount of light falling on the film per unit time. Therefore, halving the exposure time will reduce the total amount of light entering through the aperture to the original setting.

b i

f-stop	Exposure Time (s)
4	$\frac{1}{15}$
2.8	$\frac{1}{30}$
2	$\frac{1}{60}$
1.4	$\frac{1}{125}$

b ii

f-stop	Exposure Time (s)
5.6	$\frac{1}{8}$
8	$\frac{1}{4}$
11	$\frac{1}{2}$
16	1

c i

f-stop	Exposure Time (s)
5.6	$\frac{1}{125}$
8	$\frac{1}{60}$
11	$\frac{1}{30}$
16	$\frac{1}{15}$

c ii

f-stop	Exposure Time (s)
4	$\frac{1}{250}$
2.8	$\frac{1}{500}$
2	$\frac{1}{1000}$
1.4	$\frac{1}{2000}$

c iii

f-stop	Exposure Time (s)
16	$\frac{1}{4}$
11	$\frac{1}{8}$
8	$\frac{1}{15}$
5.6	$\frac{1}{30}$
4	$\frac{1}{60}$

c iv Exposure time (s): $\frac{1}{125}$

c v f-stop: f/16

c vi f-stop: f/4

5 **a i** f/1

a ii Most cameras do not have f/1.

b Yes; she could use faster film (see Investigation Five).

4 **a**

f-stop	Exposure Time (s)
8	$\frac{1}{125}$
11	$\frac{1}{60}$
16	$\frac{1}{30}$

f-stop	Exposure Time (s)
5.6	$\frac{1}{250}$
4	$\frac{1}{500}$
2	$\frac{1}{1000}$

b f/2.8 and $\frac{1}{1000}$ s; this combination would reduce blurring by using the shortest available exposure time.

c i

f-stop	Exposure Time (s)
16	$\frac{1}{30}$
11	$\frac{1}{60}$
8	$\frac{1}{125}$
5.6	$\frac{1}{250}$
4	$\frac{1}{500}$

c ii

f-stop	Exposure Time (s)
16	$\frac{1}{15}$
11	$\frac{1}{30}$
8	$\frac{1}{60}$
5.6	$\frac{1}{125}$
4	$\frac{1}{250}$

Investigation Two – Lenses

2 **a** AC represents one of the sun's rays, all of which pass through the focal point, F.

b Light rays that hit a lens at a 90° angle pass through the glass without being bent. All rays passing through a lens near its center enter and exit at nearly 90° and therefore are not bent very much.

c X'O = 120 mm (distance of B'A' from the center of the lens)

d i X'O = 60 mm

d ii X'O = 80 mm

d iii X'O = 45 mm

d iv X'O = 75 mm

f As u gets very large ($\rightarrow \infty$), $\frac{1}{u}$ gets very small ($\rightarrow 0$), leaving $\frac{1}{v} = \frac{1}{f}$ and $v = f$.

3 **a** To ensure that the image and the film are coplanar (in the same plane).

b 60 mm (300 mm also works).

Investigation Three – Depth of Field

1 **a** The photo on the left (taken at f/16). Notice that in both photos, the person in the foreground is in focus, so the person is the subject of the photograph.

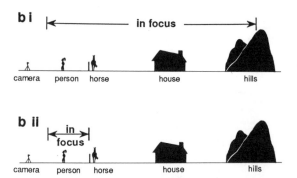

b i in focus

camera person horse house hills

b ii in focus

camera person horse house hills

2 a To ensure that the image is in focus. Note that in practice, a single simple lens as shown in Diagram 1 is not capable of accurately focusing the entire scene. Complex combinations of multiple lenses are used to improve performance in expensive cameras.

b Blurred (out of focus). Note that inexpensive cameras are designed so that the average amateur photographer barely notices the blurring with standard postcard-size enlargements. However, big enlargements will be unacceptably blurred. The professional photographer must therefore use quality lenses.

d One idea would be to photograph a detailed map with the aperture wide open for each lens. We could then order the quality of the lenses by the amount of blurring in the photos.

e In Diagram 3, the rays of light that leave D are shown as a flat bundle of rays. In fact this bundle is a three-dimensional *cone* of light rays that are bent as they pass through the lens to meet at D′ in front of the film, and then hit the film plane as a small cone of light rays once again. The cross-section of this cone is a circle; therefore D appears as a circle on the film, not a dot. This is why the image appears blurred.

f Blurred (out of focus)

g In **e,** the circle that D becomes on the film is significantly bigger than the corresponding circle. D will be much less blurred when a smaller aperture is used.

h Point E′ is behind the film, so E will also appear as a circle on the film, the light rays from E having not yet come together at a point.

i Reducing the aperture will reduce the size of the circle that represents the blurred image of point E.

j Consider a theoretically perfect lens, that is, one that can focus a point A in front of the camera on to a single point A′. (Such lenses are not possible to make.) Now any point B, either in front of or behind A, cannot be in focus on the film since B′ is not in the film's plane. However, the human eye will consider B′ to be in focus, provided the dot representing B′ is no wider than

0.2 mm on the eventual photograph. Thus there will be a range on either side of A in which B can be situated so that B′ will still appear to be in focus to the human eye. This is the depth of field. From problem **2,** it is clear that reducing the aperture reduces the diameter of the circle produced by B. We can look at this another way by noting that points further from A have their circles on the film reduced to an acceptable 0.2 mm on the resulting photograph; that is, the depth of field widens as the aperture is narrowed.

3 As the aperture is reduced, the image circle of points in front of and behind an object are reduced so that these points, as well as the object itself, appear in focus to the human eye.

Investigation Four – Patterns in the f-Stops

1 a Yes
b i Multiply one f-stop by $\sqrt{2}$ to get the next one.
b ii A single f-stop change either halves or doubles the area of the aperture. A linear scale factor of $\sqrt{2}$ (for diameter of the aperture) produces an area scale factor of 2 (doubling area).

2 a i A single stop down doubles the area of the aperture.
a ii

f-stop	Area of Aperture (mm^2)	Diameter of Aperture (mm)	Focal Length ÷ Diameter of Aperture
1.4	984	35.395871	1.4
2	492	25.028661	2.0
2.8	246	17.697936	2.8
4	123	12.514330	4.0
5.6	61.5	8.8489678	5.7
8	30.75	6.2571652	8.0
11	15.375	4.4244839	11
16	7.6875	3.1285826	16

b f-stop: 1.4, 2, 2.8, 4, 5.7, 8, 11, 16
c f-stop = focal length ÷ diameter
d i f-stop: 2, 1.4, 11, 5.6, 4
d ii

f (mm)	d (mm)	f-stop
70	35	2
67.2	12	5.6
80	5	16
90	8.2	11
200	50	4
400	143	2.8

<table>
<tr><td colspan="2">Class Investigation</td><td align="right">Page 81</td></tr>
<tr><td>2</td><td colspan="2">The f-stop for the 200 mm lens will be 200 mm ÷ 100 mm = 2. For the 50 mm lens, the f-stop is f/2 = 50/25. So for both lenses set at f/2, the intensity of light cast on the film is the same; that is, the film will be equally exposed by both lenses.</td></tr>
<tr><td>3</td><td colspan="2">In view of the answer to 2 above, she should select f/5.66 on the telephoto lens.</td></tr>
</table>

<table>
<tr><td colspan="2">On Your Own</td><td align="right">Page 82</td></tr>
<tr><td colspan="3">Lenses with low f-stops (under 2) are expensive to manufacture, so manufacturers may make an f/1.8 lens where f/1.8 is not a full stop away from f/2. Some expensive cameras have an f-stop of f/1.</td></tr>
</table>

3 **a** Each stop down doubles the area of the aperture.

b i smaller square: 1; larger square: $\sqrt{2}$ =1.414

b ii When the scale factor for area = 2, scale factor for length = $\sqrt{2}$.

c i Flowchart is correct.

c ii The flowcharts indicate that as f-stops decrease, aperture diameter increases.

Investigation Five – Film Speed

1 **a**

Film speed (ASA) x	Light Required for Correct Exposure (units) y
25	4
50	2
100	1
200	$\frac{1}{2}$
400	$\frac{1}{4}$
800	$\frac{1}{8}$
1600	$\frac{1}{16}$

b $y = \dfrac{100}{x}$

c y: 1.3, 0.67, 0.17, 0.1

<table>
<tr><td colspan="2">On Your Own</td><td align="right">Page 83</td></tr>
<tr><td>1</td><td colspan="2">a Quality portrait and landscape pictures
b Most photographs in ordinary light conditions
c In poor light conditions or when a very short exposure time is required, e.g., sports action under floodlights</td></tr>
<tr><td>2</td><td colspan="2">Photo enlargements from fast film have a grainy quality.</td></tr>
</table>

2 **a**

ASA	DIN
25	**15°**
50	**18°**
100	21°
200	24°
400	27°
800	30°
1600	33°

b

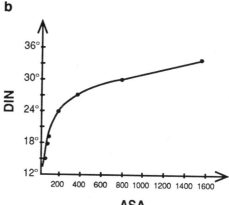

c i about 17°

c ii about 19°

c iii about 28°

f In many countries, yes

g $\frac{1}{8}$

3 **a i** To maintain correct exposure, Jody needs to double the shutter setting when the light is half the initial setting.

a ii

Fraction of Bright Light	Exposure Time (s)
1	$\frac{1}{250}$
$\frac{1}{2}$	$\frac{1}{125}$
$\frac{1}{4}$	$\frac{1}{60}$
$\frac{1}{8}$	$\frac{1}{30}$
$\frac{1}{16}$	$\frac{1}{15}$
$\frac{1}{32}$	$\frac{1}{8}$
$\frac{1}{64}$	$\frac{1}{4}$

b 200 ASA

c i

ASA	Exposure Time (s)
200	$\frac{1}{500}$
100	$\frac{1}{250}$
50	$\frac{1}{125}$
25	$\frac{1}{60}$

c ii

ASA	Exposure Time (s)
200	$\frac{1}{125}$
100	$\frac{1}{60}$
50	$\frac{1}{30}$
25	$\frac{1}{15}$

c iii

ASA	Exposure Time (s)
200	$\frac{1}{30}$
100	$\frac{1}{15}$
50	$\frac{1}{8}$
25	$\frac{1}{4}$

c iv

ASA	Exposure Time (s)
100	$\frac{1}{60}$
200	$\frac{1}{125}$
400	$\frac{1}{250}$
800	$\frac{1}{500}$

c v

ASA	Exposure Time (s)
400	$\frac{1}{4}$
800	$\frac{1}{8}$
1600	$\frac{1}{15}$
3200	$\frac{1}{30}$

c vi

ASA	Exposure Time (s)
50	$\frac{1}{15}$
100	$\frac{1}{30}$
200	$\frac{1}{60}$
400	$\frac{1}{125}$

100 ASA		200 ASA	
Light Intensity	f-stop	Light Intensity	f-stop
$\frac{1}{4}$	5.6	$\frac{1}{4}$	8
$\frac{1}{2}$	8	$\frac{1}{2}$	11
1	11	1	16

5 a i

ASA	f-stop
200	8
100	5.6
50	4
25	2.8

a ii

ASA	f-stop
200	8
400	11
800	16
1600	22

b f/5.6

Investigation
Six – Professional Photography

1 **a** The f-stop is greater.
b To record all the action, in focus, over a wide range of distances from the camera.
c Movement requires fast shutter speed.
d To maintain short exposure time and a wider depth of field when the light is poor.
e Every film has grains of silver that form the black parts on the negative. Fast film has larger grains than slow film, which means that under enlargement, the grains in fast film are much more noticeable. The graininess of slow film for similar enlargements is not nearly as noticeable, so slow film is used for portraits, which people often have enlarged.

2 **a** By increasing one f-stop from f/2.8 to f/4, he has halved the area of the aperture. He must therefore double the exposure time to $\frac{1}{30}$ s to compensate.

b

f-stop	Exposure Time (s)
1.4	$\frac{1}{250}$
2	$\frac{1}{125}$
2.8	$\frac{1}{60}$
4	$\frac{1}{30}$
5.6	$\frac{1}{15}$
8	$\frac{1}{8}$
11	$\frac{1}{4}$

4 **a i** 400 ASA
a ii No, since changing film in the middle of using a roll is impractical.
b i Because the light intensity is only one-fourth of the required value, Yoshio must multiply the area of the aperture by 4. This is achieved by moving two f-stops, from f/8 to f/5.6 to f/4.
b ii It has decreased.
b iii Yes, provided the decrease in the depth of field resulting from the change in f-stops is not a problem.

c

25 ASA		50 ASA	
Light Intensity	f-stop	Light Intensity	f-stop
$\frac{1}{4}$	2.8	$\frac{1}{4}$	4
$\frac{1}{2}$	4	$\frac{1}{2}$	5.6
1	5.6	1	8

c f/1.4 at $\frac{1}{250}$

d f/11 at $\frac{1}{4}$

e The exposure time is so long, a hand-held camera would likely result in a blurred photo.

3 **a i**

ASA	f-stop	Exposure Time (s)
400	8	$\frac{1}{60}$
200	8	$\frac{1}{30}$
100	8	$\frac{1}{15}$
50	8	$\frac{1}{8}$
50	5.6	$\frac{1}{15}$
50	8	$\frac{1}{8}$
50	11	$\frac{1}{4}$
50	16	$\frac{1}{2}$

a ii

ASA	f-stop	Exposure Time (s)
400	8	$\frac{1}{60}$
200	5.6	$\frac{1}{60}$
100	4	$\frac{1}{60}$
50	2.8	$\frac{1}{60}$
100	2.8	$\frac{1}{125}$
200	2.8	$\frac{1}{250}$
400	2.8	$\frac{1}{500}$
800	2.8	$\frac{1}{1000}$

b 396 different combinations

CHAPTER FOUR – CHECK-UP

1 **a** 4.25 mm
b i The depth of field is very large.
b ii It is good for landscapes, in which everything should be in focus.

2 **a i** $\frac{1}{4}$
a ii 2
b ASA 1 600

3 **a** $\frac{1}{30}$ s

b i $\frac{1}{15}$ s

b ii She would need a tripod, because the shutter speed is too long for a hand-held camera.
c The fastest film available (high ASA), to record all the action in focus over a wide range of distances.

CHAPTER 5   GENETICS

Investigation One – Inheritance

1 **b** Possible children of Rachel and Jack:

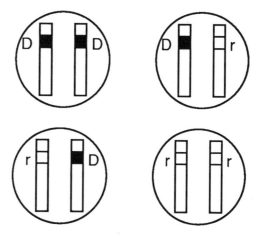

c Only *rr* will ensure a thin-faced baby, and there is 1 chance in 4 that this will occur.

2 **a**

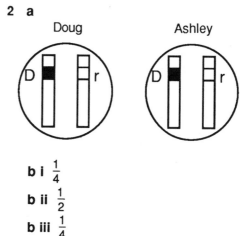

Doug   Ashley

b i $\frac{1}{4}$

b ii $\frac{1}{2}$

b iii $\frac{1}{4}$

3 b Both Heidi and Todd carry Rh– recessively.
c Yes
d No. Deirdre and Sean are both Rh– and since Rh– is recessive, neither carries the Rh+ factor, so all their children are Rh–.

4 a The gene for freckles is dominant. Todd has no freckles and so has recessive genes G_fG_f only.
b Heidi has freckles, so at least one of the genes in her chromosome pair must be G_F. She can be G_FG_F or G_FG_f.
c Two of the four possible outcomes include the dominant G_F, so the probability that a child will have freckles is 2 out of 4 or $\frac{1}{2}$.

d i

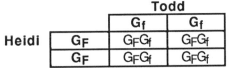

	Todd	
	G_f	G_f
Heidi G_F	G_FG_f	G_FG_f
G_F	G_FG_f	G_FG_f

d ii 1
e The correct table is Erika's (in **c**).

5 a

	Father	
	G_t	G_t
Mother G_T	G_TG_t	G_TG_t
G_t	G_tG_t	G_tG_t

b $\frac{1}{2}$

c i

	Father	
	G_T	G_t
Mother G_t	G_TG_t	G_tG_t
G_t	G_TG_t	G_tG_t

c ii $\frac{1}{2}$

6 a Since the gene for thin lips is recessive, anyone with thin lips is G_lG_l. Therefore Howard received G_l from his father and, because he has thick lips, received the dominant G_L from his mother. His mother is either G_LG_L or G_LG_l. If his mother were G_LG_l, on average one-half of her children would be thin lipped. Since all six children have thick lips, she is almost certainly G_LG_L.
b This follows from the answer in problem **6 a**.
c 3

7 a $\frac{1}{2}$
b $\frac{1}{4}$

Investigation Two – Blood Types

1 a

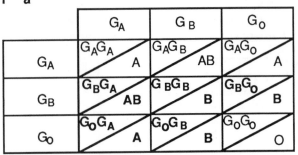

	G_A	G_B	G_O
G_A	G_AG_A A	G_AG_B AB	G_AG_O A
G_B	G_BG_A AB	G_BG_B B	G_BG_O B
G_O	G_OG_A A	G_OG_B B	G_OG_O O

b i Blood type A requires at least one of the gene pairings to be G_A. The other gene can be either G_O or G_A.
b ii G_BG_B or G_BG_O
b iii Possible blood types for Ross and Jocelyn's children:

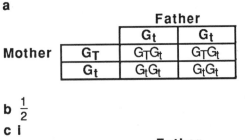

(AB) (A) (AB) (A)

b iv

		G_AG_A		G_AG_O	
		G_A	G_A	G_A	G_O
G_BG_B	G_B	G_BG_A	G_BG_A	G_BG_A	G_BG_O
	G_B	G_BG_A	G_BG_A	G_BG_A	G_BG_O
G_BG_O	G_B	G_BG_A	G_BG_A	G_BG_A	G_BG_O
	G_O	G_OG_A	G_OG_A	G_OG_A	G_OG_O

b v A child with blood type O has G_OG_O. From the table, Ross must be G_AG_O and Jocelyn must be G_BG_O.
c i AB blood can only come from G_AG_B. Having blood type B might mean that G_O is present recessively; that is, Richard might be G_BG_O. Blood type B can also be G_BG_B.

		G_BG_B		G_BG_O	
		G_B	G_B	G_B	G_O
G_AG_B	G_A	G_AG_B	G_AG_B	G_AG_B	G_AG_O
	G_B	G_BG_B	G_BG_B	G_BG_B	G_BG_O

c ii A child with blood type A is G_AG_A or G_AG_O. G_AG_A is not possible, so the child is G_AG_O. Look for G_AG_O in the table and notice it is in the right hand side, so Richard must be G_BG_O

d Any child of Bill must be G_AG_B, G_AG_O, or G_BG_O.

e If Dawn is G_AG_O and Steve is G_BG_O, the proba-bility they have a child with O blood type is $\frac{1}{4}$. So in claiming that he is adopted, the son *may* be correct. If Steve is G_BG_B, his claim is correct.

2 **a** Genes of father: G_OG_O, G_AG_O, G_OG_O, G_OG_O; genes of mother: G_AG_O, G_BG_O, G_OG_O, G_BG_O or G_BG_B

b i Father G_AG_O, mother G_AG_B

b ii Father G_OG_A, mother G_BG_O

b iii Father G_OG_A, mother almost certainly G_BG_B, with a small probability that she is G_BG_O

3 The data indicate that "waves" of peoples of different blood types move from (perhaps) Southeast Asia through Indonesia and Papua New Guinea to Australia. Those Australian Aborigines nearest Papua New Guinea (Cape York), which is the likely point of entry to Australia, intermarry with the newcomers and their descendants tend to take on their blood types. Aboriginals farther away from the points of immediate contact (Central Australia and the Western Desert) will inherit new proportions of blood types very slowly because of their remoteness from the point of contact.

Investigation
Three – Inherited Diseases

1 **a i**

Woody Guthrie

		G_H	G_h
Arlo's	G_h	G_hG_H	G_hG_h
mother	G_h	G_hG_H	G_hG_h

a ii $\frac{1}{2}$

b You might not want to know that you have Huntington's chorea, as this informs you of your certan early death. On the other hand, you might want to know for certain whether you have it so that you can plan whether to have children.

c i

Clara

		G_H	G_h
Patrick	G_h	G_hG_H	G_hG_h
	G_h	G_hG_H	G_hG_h

c ii

Clara

		G_h	G_h
Patrick	G_h	G_hG_h	G_hG_h
	G_h	G_hG_h	G_hG_h

d $\frac{2}{8}$ or $\frac{1}{4}$

e $\frac{1}{2}$

On Your Own   **Page 104**

Suppose K and L are first cousins. K has Huntington's chorea. Their family tree back to their possible six grandparents will be like this:

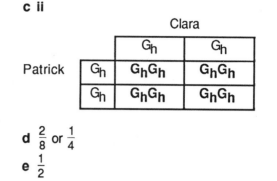

K and L share grandparents C and D. Family history will probably show whether K got the disease from G or H. If it is from G, L will be in the clear. If it is from H (that is, C or D has the disease), then I may also have it. But in this case it is almost certain that if L is about the same age as K, I will be old enough to be clear, in which case L will also be clear. If I died at a relatively early age, L may not be in the clear and more information will be necessary to determine the probability that L has the disease.

2 **a** Yes

b Yes

c Frances's father is already 50 and is free of the disease, so Frances will not get it from her father's side.

d No. Her maternal grandfather died at 28 before showing signs of the disease and *his* mother died at 24, also before showing signs of the disease.

e Cynthia Smith, Marilyn Morton, Patricia McLeod, Colin McLeod (although he is likely to be clear, because he is past the age by which most sufferers show symptoms), and perhaps Vera Smith—*if* her father died young.

f Huntington's chorea is a degenerative disease, and families may deny its existence out of embarrassment; or, carriers of the disease may have died before the disease became apparent.

---

3 b

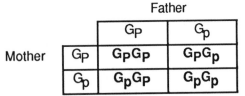

Father

Mother		G_P	G_p
	G_P	G_PG_P	G_PG_p
	G_p	G_pG_P	G_pG_p

c Both parents must be carriers, which is very unlikely (about 1 chance in 6400).

4 a The child receives the sickle-cell anemia from both parents.
b She knows that 1 in 100 sets of Black American parents can produce children with sickle-cell anemia, but there is 1 chance in 4 that this will happen. Thus there is 1 chance in 400 that Black American couples will have a child with the disease.

5 a When a carrier from group A marries a carrier from group B, there is a 1 in 4 chance that they will have a child with McGill's disease and not just a carrier.
b Intermarriage between close relatives will increase the spread of inherited diseases.
d They could prohibit marriages between people from the community.

Investigation
Four – Gender-Linked Diseases

1 a X_hX_H is a girl who has both the clotting and non-clotting factors. The clotting factor is dominant, so the girl is a carrier of hemophilia.
b i A female who is not a carrier
b ii A male who is not a hemophiliac
b iii A male suffering from hemophilia
c Even minor cuts or bruising often led to death.
d i

	X_H	X_H
X_h	X_hX_H	X_hX_H
Y	X_HY	X_HY

d ii From the table, any son has X_H from the mother.
d iii From the table, any daughter is X_hX_H, i.e., carries X_h recessively.
e

	X_H	X_h
X_h		X_hX_h
Y		

The girl X_hX_h is a hemophiliac.

2 a Statements **i, iii, iv, v, vii,** and **viii** are either true or almost certainly true.
b They were shot by the Bolsheviks before having children.
3 a Possible children of Dorothy and Fletcher:

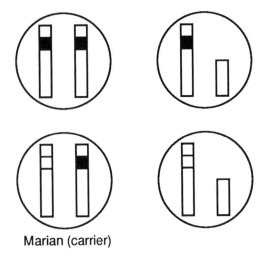

Marian (carrier)

b Possible children of Andrew and Heather:

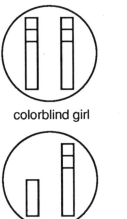

colorblind girl   carrier girl

colorblind boy   normal boy

c Yes
d $\frac{1}{2}$

CHAPTER 5 – CHECK-UP

1 a Recessive
b No, because both Emily and her husband are G_CG_C, where G_C is the recessive gene for a concave nose.
2 One parent is blood type A and the other is blood type B.
3 Yes, because blue eyes are recessive.

3 Yes, because blue eyes are recessive.

4

Teresa

Ian		G_H	G_h
	G_H	$G_H G_H$	$G_H G_h$
	G_h	$G_h G_H$	$G_h G_h$

Each outcome is equally likely, so there is a probability of 1 in 4 or 25% that their child will be $G_h G_h$ (thus having straight hair).

5 **a** It is recessive. If it were dominant, a person would die before reaching sexual maturity.
b One in 625 sets of Caucasian parents can produce children with cystic fibrosis, but there is 1 chance in 4 that such couples will have a child with the disease. Thus there is 1 chance in 2500 that Caucasians will produce a child with cystic fibrosis.
c $\frac{1}{4}$

6 **a** Death usually occurs before the sufferers reproduce, so there are no children to pass on the dominant disorder.
b Huntington's chorea continues to exist because it begins to affect the sufferer in middle age.

7 **a** For a girl to have Lum's syndrome, it would be necessary for both parents to have the condition. While this is possible for the mother, the father would have died in childhood with the disease.
b i Say that X_L is the gene for not having Lum's syndrome (dominant) and X_l is the gene for having the disease (recessive). If the father is $X_L Y$ and the mother is $X_L X_l$, then the possible outcomes are $X_L X_L$, $X_L Y$, $X_l X_L$ or $X_l Y$.

b ii $\frac{1}{4}$